Many Witnesses, One Lord

William Barclay

Westminster John Knox Press
LOUISVILLE
LONDON · LEIDEN

Published in the U.S.A. in 2001 by
Westminster John Knox Press
Louisville, Kentucky

Original edition published in English under the title
Many Witnesses, One Lord by John Hunt Publishing Ltd.,
46a West Street, New Alresford, Hants, UK.

PRINTED IN HONG KONG

01 02 03 04 05 06 07 08 09 10 — 10 9 8 7 6 5 4 3 2 1

Library of Congress Cataloging-in-Publication Data
Barclay, William, 1907-1978.
    Many witnesses, one Lord / William Barclay.
        p. cm.
    Originally published: Philadelphia: Westminister Press, 1963.
    ISBN 0-664-22387-7 (alk. paper)
    1. Bible. N.T.--Criticism, interpretation, etc. I. Title.

BS2361.3.B375 2001
225.6-dc2l

                                                            00-065476

Contents

Preface

This book has been written to say something that I have long felt, and long wished to say. We have heard much of the unity of the New Testament, and that unity is something which no one will wish to deny. But in the New Testament there is also diversity. There is no one standardized religious experience; there is no one stereotyped interpretation of the Christian faith and message. There is a company of men witnessing to what Jesus Christ has been to them, and still is. It is in the mercy of God that there are many ways to God, for in the many-colored grace of God a man will find that which will match his need. So in this book I have tried to see what Christ and Christianity and the Christian life meant to the different men who wrote the books of the New Testament.

It is therefore true that the most obvious thing about this book is that it attempted the impossible. He who writes for a series of books of uniform length must abide within the strait-jacket of his allotted space. And so to try to describe the diversity of the New Testament in rather less than forty thousand words is the task with which the writer is confronted.

This has necessarily meant selection, and inevitably other people would have selected other things. How can one write of the message of the Synoptic Gospels in a few pages? Why should one choose the first chapter of John as central and not the fourteenth and the sixteenth, or the fifteenth and the seventeenth? But choice had to be made, and in the end choice is personal. And if, indeed, my choice drives the reader to make his choice, then the aim of this book will have been achieved.

It is my hope and my prayer that this book may do something to send its readers to the New Testament themselves that there they may find in its rich diversity that which speaks directly to their heart and to their need.

WILLIAM BARCLAY

1

Many Ways to God

That great teacher and saint A. J. Gossip used to have a favorite saying. Often he would say that there are not four Gospels but five. There are the Gospels according to Matthew, Mark, Luke and John, and there is the Gospel according to a man's own experience – and the fifth is the most important of all. It was not enough for the disciples to be able to tell Jesus what others said and thought of him. The basic and essential and all-important question was: '*You* – who do *you* say that I am?' (Matthew 16.13-16). A man may be an expert able to pass an examination on all Christologies ancient and modern, but the real question is not what Jesus Christ meant to Irenaeus or Origen, Anselm or Aquinas, Luther or Calvin, Ritschl or Macleod Campbell, Barth or Aulén, but: 'What does the Gospel mean to *you*?' God does not treat men as mass-produced, identical repetitions one of another; he treats men as individuals, no two of whom are alike. 'God', as it has been said, 'has his own secret stairway into every heart.' 'There are as many ways to the stars as there are men to climb them.' 'God', as Tennyson said, 'fulfils himself in many ways.'

In what follows we shall go on to think of the Gospel in the Synoptic Gospels, in John, in Paul, in Peter, in James, in Hebrews, in the letters of John, in II Peter and in Jude, and in the Revelation; but it is of the first importance to remember that we are not dealing with a series of Gospels competing with one another for our allegiance. The different expressions of the Gospel are not competing and antithetic; they are co-operative and complementary.

1

Although we do not mean ourselves to use the classification, it is of interest to note that it has been said that broadly speaking there are four different types of religion presented in the NT.

1. There is the conception of religion as inward fellowship with God, resulting in a union so close that the believer can speak of himself as *in Christ*, and can say that it is no longer he who lives but Christ who lives in him. That is the characteristic experience of Paul.

2. There is the conception of religion as a right way of life, a right standard of living, and the inspiration to attempt, and the power to reach, that kind of life. That is the characteristic experience of James and Peter.

3. There is the conception of religion as the highest satisfaction of a man's mind, the truth to which he reaches out, and which by the help of the Spirit of God he grasps, and in which he rests. That is the characteristic experience of John.

4. There is the conception of religion as access and approach to God, in which a man enters out of the shadows into the light, out of the passing things of time into eternity, out of the world into the presence of God. That is the characteristic experience of the writer to the Hebrews.

It may well be that there are two things to which we do not ordinarily attach enough importance.

1. There is the effect of a man's personal experience of life upon his religion. It is always true that we only grasp those parts of the truth which we are compelled to grasp. There are things which we know well enough with our minds, but which only the compulsion of experience can make part of our very lives. I do not think, for instance, that the idea of the life beyond death ever becomes vividly and intensely real to us until someone we loved has died. Clearly, there will be a difference between the experience of the man who from his childhood days had known and loved Jesus, who has never had any real doubts, who has

never, so to speak, been away from home, and the experience of
the man to whom Jesus Christ is a new discovery, who has
wandered in the deserts of infidelity, who has stained and
blotted his life, who has been in the far countries of the soul. It
is out of experience that faith is born, and a man's experience
will color his faith.

2. There is the effect of a man's temperament on his
religion. There are those who are by nature placid and even
lethargic, and there are tempestuous beings whose passions are
at white heat and whose temper is on a hair trigger. There are
those who are constitutionally disposed to accept things and to
whom the blue waters never call, and there are those who must
understand or perish and who must ever adventure on the
uncharted seas of thought. Clearly, the difference in
temperament will beget a difference in the experience of
religion.

There is a word which the NT uses to describe the grace of
God, the word *poikilos* (I Peter 4.10); the AV translates it
manifold; the RSV and the NEB translate it *varied*. It really
means *many-colored*; and the idea is that there is no color in the
human situation which the grace of God cannot match.
Whatever be a man's experience, whatever be a man's
temperament, Jesus Christ has that which can meet man's need.

This is the thought with which this book is written. We have
of late years heard much about the unity of the NT, and to that
we will in the end come; but there is a strong case for thinking
sometimes of the diversity of the NT. We are not seeking to
present the NT as a series of contradictory and competing
Gospels; we are trying to see how those who wrote it were
witnessing to what Jesus Christ meant to them so that we may
be moved to see what Jesus Christ means to us.

2
The Synoptic Gospels

The Gospel of the Kingdom

The Synoptic Gospels by Mark, Matthew and Luke leave us in no doubt concerning the message with which Jesus came. Jesus came preaching the Gospel of God: 'The time is fulfilled, and the Kingdom of God is at hand; repent, and believe the Gospel' (Mark 1.15).

Here is the conception of the Kingdom. This was not a new conception, but it was a fluid conception. To a Pharisee the Kingdom was a time when men would perfectly obey the Law. 'If Israel would only keep the Law perfectly for one day the Kingdom would come.' On the whole the Sadducees were not much interested in the Kingdom; their main preoccupation was to keep things as they were, so that by a policy of prudent collaboration they might retain their wealth and their political influence. The quiet in the land thought of the Kingdom in terms of quiet devotion to God, in prayer to him, waiting for him, and communion with him. No doubt the great mass of the people thought of the Kingdom in terms of national deliverance, liberation and power. They could cite the prophets.

> I will make your oppressors eat their own flesh,
>> And they shall be drunk with their own blood as with wine.
>
> *(Isaiah 49.26)*

> For the nation and the kingdom
>> that will not serve you shall perish;
>> those nations shall be utterly laid waste.
>
> *(Isaiah 60.12)*

4

With the conception of the Kingdom there was indissolubly connected the idea of the Messiah, the champion of God who would deliver the people of God; and Jesus accepted the confession of faith of Peter at Caesarea Philippi: 'You are the Messiah, the Son of the living God' (Matthew 16.16, NEB). Again the idea of the Messiah was fluid, and might mean either a mighty human champion of David's line, or a divine supernatural figure unleashed by God in irresistible might upon the world.

Still further, and again inextricably connected with the Kingdom and the Messiah, was the conception of the Day of the Lord. It was the increasing conviction of the Jews that things had come to such a pass that the Kingdom could never come by human means. They therefore divided time into two ages, this present age, which is wholly and incurably bad, and the age to come, which is the blessed age of God. The time between was the Day of the Lord when God would suddenly and shatteringly break into the world in cosmos-destroying power and judgment, and in which the old world would be completely destroyed and the new world born.

Into this complex of ideas Jesus came, and he came preaching the Kingdom. The word kingdom tends to mean to us an area of land ruled over by a king; in the NT the word rather means the Reign of God. It describes not an area of territory but the universal sovereignty of God. The odd thing is that Jesus never defined the Kingdom. We can be perfectly sure that he did not think of in terms of the observance of the Law or in terms of national empire. How then did he think of it? He taught men to pray:

Thy Kingdom come,
Thy will be done,
  On earth as it is in heaven.

(Matthew 6.10)

If we apply to that the principle of Hebrew parallelism in which the second arm of the two parallel phrases reiterates or explains the first, then we can say that the *Kingdom is a society upon earth in which God's will is as perfectly done as it is in heaven.* And this makes good sense, for any kingdom is both an area and a society in which the king's word is law. If this be so, it sets us at once in two relationships.

1. It sets us in *a relationship to God*; and that relationship is *obedience*. If we then equate the membership of the Kingdom with the acceptance of the will of God, we find that the Kingdom is worth everything a man has to give (Matthew 13.44, 45). The acceptance of the will of God is worth any sacrifice, however surgical, that a man may be called upon to make (Mark 9.43-48). For the Christian the most important thing in the universe is the will of God. Only when he accepts that will is he in the Kingdom.

2. But clearly, the citizens of a kingdom are not only in a relationship to their king, they are also in *a relationship to each other*. So membership of the Kingdom demands a certain attitude to our fellow men.

(*a*) It demands a certain *usefulness*. Uselessness invites disaster (Luke 13.6-9), and the failure to use the talents God has given brings judgment (Matthew 25.14-30). So far from detaching a man from the world the Kingdom sets him firmly in it.

(*b*) It demands an attitude of *mercy*. It is only the merciful who will receive mercy (Matthew 5.7), and only the forgiving who can be forgiven (Matthew 18.23-35). So far from equipping a man with a consciously superior and intolerant goodness the Kingdom must equip a man with a sympathy as wide as the world.

(*c*) We may put this more widely. Membership of the Kingdom means *the deepest possible involvement in the human situation* (Matthew 25.31-46). Citizenship of the Kingdom involves a new sense of responsibility; it joins a man as firmly to his fellow-men as it joins him to God.

(*d*) All this means to say that *the law of the Kingdom is love.* The watchword of the Kingdom is that untranslatable word *agapē*, that unconquerable benevolence, that determination to seek nothing but the highest good of all men, that reflection of God's attitude to men.

In the Kingdom love of God and love of men go hand in hand. Obedience to God is paramount and no fine words can ever be a substitute for it (Matthew 7.21-23); involvement with men is essential and no one who passes by on the other side can be a member of the Kingdom (Luke 10.29-37).

In the Synoptic Gospels the Kingdom is conceived of in a double way. It is conceived of as a *growth*. It is a slow, steady, unseen growth, developing not by the effort of man, but by the power of God (Mark 4.26-29); Matthew 13.33). In this sense the Kingdom might well be called the product of the power and Spirit of God at work in the world and in the minds and hearts of men. But it is also conceived of as a *consummation* (Matthew 24; Mark 13). It is not, as it were, a growth which will never be anything else but a growth; it is a growth moving towards a consummation in which at last the will of God will be done not partially but completely, and in which the kingdoms of the world will become the Kingdom of God. Quite inevitably that involves judgment, for where there must be obedience there can be disobedience, and where there is a king who lays claim to the world there must be rebels who refuse his claim.

Wherein then is Jesus' place within this Kingdom? First and foremost, Jesus *is* the Kingdom, Jesus *embodied* the Kingdom. If the Kingdom is a state and condition of things in which the will of God is perfectly accepted and done, then Jesus is the only person in the universe who perfectly accepted that will. The thread that binds the life of Jesus together is his continual acceptance of the will of God. At the beginning and the end of his life on earth we see him accepting that will. In the temptation story (Matthew 4.1-11; Luke 4.1-13) we see him accepting that way which can end only in the Cross. In Gethsemane (Matthew 26.36-46; Mark 14.32-42; Luke 22.39-46) we see him still accepting this will. In Jesus the Kingdom actually and in fact *did* come. To look at him is to see life in the Kingdom.

But the Synoptic Gospels do not leave the matter there. If this was all that we could say, then there could descend on the human spirit nothing but blank despair, for all that this does is to present us with a picture of the impossible. The necessary obedience is something that no man can ever bring, and to think of the Kingdom in terms of obedience is to think of it in terms of judgment which no man could escape. It would be in fact to make law the moving and dominating conception in the Kingdom.

When we lay down obedience as the principle of the Kingdom, when we lay down as the all-important decision the acceptance of the will of God, we are immediately faced with another question. What is the attitude behind that will of God? What is the character, what is the heart, of which that will is the expression? If that will is heartless, if that will is tyrannical and capricious, if that will is harsh and even cruel, then it may have to be accepted, but the acceptance can only be the act of a man who knows that he is crushed into helplessness and can do no other. He may accept it, but his acceptance will be either the acceptance of defeated resignation or rebellious resentment. That cannot be so, because Jesus came preaching the *Gospel* of God and urging men to repent and believe in the *Gospel*, and the Gospel is literally Good News (Mark 1.14, 15). What, then, is this Good News?

It is Good News about God, and it is summed up in the name

which Jesus taught men to use to God, and the name by which he taught men to think of God. That name is Father. It is more than that; it is *Abba* (Mark 14.36; Romans 8.15; Galatians 4.6). This is the name by which a little child called his father in the home-circle in Palestine, as *jaba* still is in Arabic today. It is the name the picture of which is drawn in the parable of the prodigal son (Luke 15.11-32), which would be far better called the parable of the loving Father. It is quite true that in the OT God is called the father of the nation and even the father of the king; but nowhere is there this individualized fatherhood which Jesus taught us is the supreme characteristic of God.

The very name changes the whole atmosphere. So long as we think in terms of a kingdom we have to think in terms of a king; and in the conception of kingship there is always something remote and distant and withdrawn. It is only to very few that it can ever be given to be on intimate terms with a king, or who can hope to have at any time unhindered access to the presence of the king. But as soon as the word father is mentioned the picture changes from that of a kingdom to a family; and thereby our relationship to God is completely changed. The essence of the divine – human relationship becomes not law but love. Sin becomes not a breaking of God's law but a breaking of God's heart. The desire of the penitent sinner becomes not flight from the king and judge but return to the father who waits in patient love. The very essence of this relationship is expressed in Jesus' lamentation over Jerusalem: 'O Jerusalem, Jerusalem, killing the prophets and stoning those who are sent to you! How often would I have gathered your children together as a hen gathers her brood under her wings, and you would not' (Matthew 23.37). There speaks the voice, not of outraged majesty, not of insulted law, but of yearning love.

And where does Jesus come into this in the thought of the Synoptic Gospels? He comes into it in a double way.

1. Apart from Jesus men could never have known that God is like this. It was easy and natural and instinctive to think of him as King and Judge; it was far too good to be true to think of him as waiting and yearning love. Jesus is the Son of God; and, whatever else that may mean, and however else that relationship may be defined, it certainly does mean that the relationship between Jesus and God is so close and essential and intimate that Jesus can tell men what God is really like. There is no need to guess and grope any more. Jesus knows what God is like, because he is the Son of the Father – and the message he brings is Good News.

2. But there is more to it than that. It would be easy to sentimentalize this conception of God, and to persuade one-self in consequence of it that sin does not matter; but the God who is Father does not cease to be the God who is Judge and King, and the God who is loving does not cease to be the God who is holy. Sin, therefore, matters, intensely and cannot be waved aside as if it had never existed.

Now if a Jew was to think on these lines at all, and with all his heritage he could not avoid doing so, he was bound to think in terms of sacrifice, for it was through penitence expressed in terms of sacrifice that sin could be forgiven. The Synoptic Gospels, therefore, think of Jesus as making the sacrifice of his life for the sins of the world. 'The Son of Man came to seek and to save that which was lost' (Luke 19.10). 'The Son of Man came ... to give his life a ransom for many' (Mark 10.45). It would not have entered the minds of the early preachers to discuss to whom the sacrifice was made and to whom the ransom was paid; they would simply have been firm and immovable in the conviction that it cost the death of Jesus to make it possible for men to come back home to the family of God.

The Synoptic Gospels tell of the Good News of the

Kingdom. The Kingdom means the Reign of the will of God. That Reign grows steadily but there is 'one divine far off event to which the whole creation moves'. Jesus revealed God as Father, and therefore a Father's will can be willingly and humbly and trustfully accepted, even if the cost of acceptance be very great. And the sacrifice of Jesus Christ upon the Cross dealt finally with the sin of man, and made it possible for man, the prodigal son, to enter again into the family circle of the God, who is the loving Father and the holy King.

3
John

The Gospel of the Word

To very many people the Fourth Gospel is the high-water mark of the NT. 'Chiefest of the Gospels,' Luther called it, 'unique, tender and true.' Very early in the history of the Church the four living creatures of the Revelation (4.7) were used as the symbols of the Gospels. The allocation of them varies, but according to Augustine the man stands for Mark, who gives us the most human picture of Jesus; the lion stands for Matthew, who shows us Jesus as the Messiah, the lion of Judah; the ox stands for Luke, for the ox is the animal of sacrifice, and Luke shows us Jesus as the sacrifice and the Savior for the sins of the world; and the eagle stands for John, 'because John took a higher flight, and soared in his preaching much more sublimely than the other three' (*Homilies on John*, 36). It is said that only the eagle of all living creatures can look straight into the sun; so John looks more directly into the blaze of divine truth than any other of the Gospel writers. Certain things have to be noted about John.

1. John did not write until almost AD 100. His Gospel is, therefore, the product of long thought and of long living with Jesus and of long experience of the Spirit. W. M. Macgregor has a sermon entitled *What Jesus becomes to a man who has known him long*, and that is an excellent description of John's Gospel. John was more concerned with the meaning of the facts of Jesus' life than with the facts themselves. It is in John that we get the highest teaching of the Spirit. 'I have yet many things to

say to you, but you cannot bear them now. When the Spirit of truth comes, he will guide you into all truth' (John 16. 12, 13). For John that promise had come true; he saw things that only years in the Spirit could teach; and his Gospel may well be called the Gospel of the Spirit.

2. All tradition has it that John did not write alone. The account of the writing of the Fourth Gospel in the Muratorian Canon, the earliest list of the books of the NT, cannot be factually correct, but it is certainly true in principle: 'When his fellow-disciples and bishops urged John [to write], he said: "Fast together with me for three days, and let us tell to each other what shall be revealed to each one of us." On the same night it was revealed to Andrew, one of the apostles, that, with all of them reviewing it, John should describe all things in his own name.' The picture is that of a group sitting in the Spirit and remembering and saying to each other: 'You remember what Jesus said . . . and now we know that this is what he meant.' In John we have the product of what happens when two or three are gathered together in the name of Jesus (Matthew 18.20).

3. John was confronted with a different problem from that of the other Gospel writers. They had been Jews writing in Jewish terms largely for Jews, or for those brought up in the Jewish tradition; but John was in Ephesus and he had to find some way of expressing the truth of the Gospel in a way that a Greek could understand. To call Jesus Son of David or even Messiah would be to a Greek quite unintelligible. John found his new way in the conception of Jesus as the *Logos*, the Word. This conception has three advantages.

(*a*) It has *a universal background*. In any circumstances a word is two things. First, a word is the expression of a thought. We think and then we express the thought in words. So then to call Jesus the Word is to call him the expression of the thought of God. Second, a word is a means of communication.

Therefore, to call Jesus the Word is to say that he is the person and the means whereby God communicates with men.

(b) It has *a Jewish background*. To a Jew a word was not simply a sound in the air. A word was a thing which did things; it was an effective unit of energy. A word did not only *say* things; it *did* things. If that is true of a human word, how much more it must be true of the divine word. The word of God does not return void and ineffective; it does what God designed it to do (Isaiah 55.11). The word of God is like a hammer that breaks the rocks in pieces (Jeremiah 23.29). By the word of God the heavens were made (Psalm 33.6-9). Every act of creation begins, 'And God said . . . ' (Genesis 1.3, 6, 9, 11, 14, 20, 24, 26). So then to say that Jesus is the word of God is to say that he is the dynamic, creative power of God in action.

Here we have to insert into the pattern another basic fact. *Logos* does not only mean *word*; it also means *reason*. There is in fact no English term which covers both these meanings, and that is why Moffatt in his translation does not attempt to translate it, but simply says: 'The Logos became flesh.' Now in Judaism another idea became increasingly common, the place of Wisdom, *Sophia*, in the work and design of God. In Proverbs 8.22-31 Wisdom is there from the beginning, and before the beginning, the master workman who was God's agent in the creation of the world. This is still further developed in the inter-testamental Wisdom literature. Wisdom was present at creation and was the instrument of God's creating work (Wisdom 9.1, 2, 9). Wisdom is nothing else than the breath of the power of God, and the clear effluence of the glory of the Almighty (Wisdom 7.25). Here again we have the idea of Reason, Wisdom, *Logos, Sophia* as the creative power and energy of God, existing before the world began.

(c) It has *a Greek background*. In Greek thought the *Logos* had a very special function. The Greek thinkers were impressed by the diversity of the universe, and by the principle of change and alteration which obviously operates within it. But they were also deeply impressed by the dependability of the universe, by the fact that this is a reliable universe with a pattern and a plan in it, in which all things follow in their appointed order and in which a cause always produces the same effect. So they asked, what keeps the stars in their courses, what makes the sun rise and set, what brings back the seasons in their appointed order, what is it that puts mind into man? Their answer was that this is the work of the *Logos*, the mind of God operating in the world. So then to call Jesus the *Logos* is to say that he is the mind of God, become a flesh and blood human creature. It is as if John said: 'For centuries you have been speaking and thinking about the *Logos*, the mind of God, and you have been tracing the *Logos* in the structure of the universe. If you want to see the mind of God full displayed, look at Jesus.'

(*d*) One final piece has to be fitted into the pattern. Almost at the same time as Jesus and Paul there lived in Alexandria a great Jewish thinker called Philo; he knew Jewish thought and he knew Greek thought as no one else has ever known both. He was the bridge between them. In his voluminous works there are no fewer than six hundred references to the *Logos*, and basically they all have the same essential thought. God is high and lifted up, utterly transcendent. He cannot himself communicate directly with sinful man. His means of communication, his liaison with the world is the *Logos*. 'The Father, who has begotten all things, granted as his choicest privilege to the chief messenger and most august *Logos* that he should stand in the midst between the created and the Creator.' So to say that Jesus is the *Logos* is to say that he is God's supreme means of communication with men.

So then all these lines converge on the one thought that the *Logos*, with its double meaning of word and reason, is the expression of the mind of God, and the power of God in action. In Jesus we see in human action the mind of God.

Let us now turn to the Prologue, the first 18 verses of the Fourth Gospel to see what John has to say about Jesus as the *Logos*. We find that he has five things to say.

1. He tells us *what Jesus personally was*. He begins with a brief statement which provides the translator with a problem not far from insoluble in the English language. 'The Word', say both the AV and the RSV, 'was God' (John 1.1). Moffatt is one of the few modern translators who dare to depart from that rendering. 'The Logos', he translates, 'was divine.' In a matter like this we cannot do other than go to the Greek, which is *theos ēn ho logos*. *Theos* is the Greek for *God*, *ēn* for *was*, *ho* for *the*, *logos* for *word*. Now normally, except for special reasons, Greek nouns always have the definite article in front of them, and we can see at once here that *theos* the noun for *God* has not got the definite article in front of it. When a Greek noun has not got the article in front of it, it becomes rather a description than an identification, and has the character of an adjective rather than of a noun. We can see exactly the same in English. If I say: 'James is *the* man', then I identify James with some definite man whom I have in mind; but, if I say: 'James is man', then I am simply describing James as human, and the word man has become a description and not an identification. If John had said *ho theos ēn ho logos*, using a definite article in front of both nouns, then he would definitely have identified the *logos* with God, but because he has no definite article in front of *theos* it becomes a description, and more of an adjective than a noun. The translation then becomes, to put it rather clumsily, 'The Word was in the same class as God, belonged to the same order of being as God'. The only modern translator who fairly and squarely faced this problem is Kenneth Wuest, who has: 'The Word was as to his essence essential deity.' But it is here that the

NEB has brilliantly solved the problem with the absolutely accurate rendering: 'What God was the Word was.'

John is not here identifying the Word with God. To put it very simply, he does not say that Jesus was God. What he does say is that no human description of Jesus can be adequate, and that Jesus, however you are going to define it, must be described in terms of God. 'I know men,' said Napoleon, 'and Jesus Christ is more than a man.'

But no sooner has John presented us with a problem in translation than he presents us with a problem in theology. 'In the beginning', he says, 'was the Word.' 'He was in the beginning with God' (John 1.1, 2). Here we come upon the doctrine which is known as the doctrine of the pre-existence of the Word, or the pre-existence of the Son. There is no more difficult doctrine to understand in all theological thinking. It quite clearly cannot mean that this flesh and blood man Jesus existed before the creation of the world. What then does it mean?

We do not say that in what follows there is anything like a full account of the meaning of the pre-existence of the Son or of the Word, but, whatever else that doctrine may or may not mean, it does mean this. Let us remind ourselves what John basically means when he called Jesus the Word; he meant that in Jesus we see perfectly displayed in human form the mind of God. To put it at its very simplest, he meant that God is like Jesus. This means that, when we see Jesus feeding the hungry and healing the sick and being the friend of outcasts and sinners, when we see Jesus dying on the Cross, we can say: 'God is like that.' Now, if we go on to speak of the pre-existence of the *Logos*, one thing at least that we must mean is that *God was always like that*. The mind of God, the attitude of God towards men, was always from all eternity to all eternity that which we see in Jesus.

To grasp this is of the most crucial importance. There are certain ways of speaking about Jesus which imply, or even come near to stating, that Jesus did something to change the attitude of God to men, that somehow Jesus changed God's wrath into love, that somehow Jesus persuaded God to hold his hand and to pacify his anger and to withhold his judgment of condemnation, that, to put it very crudely, Jesus by his sufferings and his death bought off God. It is perfectly possible to speak in such a way as to leave an impression of an opposition and a contrast between Jesus and God. Jesus is presented as forgiving love; God is presented as awful holiness; and Jesus is depicted as winning forgiveness for men from God.

But, if we insist that the *Logos* was in the beginning and before the beginning, it means very simply that God was always like Jesus and always will be, and that Jesus did not come to change the attitude of God to men, but to show quite unmistakably what that attitude is and always was.

2. John goes on to tell us *what Jesus did*. 'All things were made by him, and without him was not anything made that was made' (John 1.3). The Word, the Son, Jesus is thus connected with the creation of the world, which for a modern mind has always been a difficult idea, and yet an idea integral to NT thought. 'By him', says Paul, 'all things were created, that are in heaven and that are in earth, visible and invisible' (Colossians 1.16). The writer to the Hebrews speaks of the Son by whom God made the worlds (Hebrews 1.2). Paul speaks of the Lord Jesus Christ by whom are all things (I Corinthians 8.6).

The connection of the Word, the Son, with creation was an idea which arose to combat a certain heresy which we shall meet again as we study other NT books. In the Graeco-Roman world there was a type of thought which goes by the general name of Gnosticism. Gnosticism sought to explain the evil in the world by means of a thorough-going dualism. It said that from all eternity there has been in the world two realities, Spirit, which is God, and matter. Spirit and matter are co-eternal. Matter is the stuff, the raw material, out of which the world is made, and from the beginning matter is essentially flawed and imperfect. This is to say that the world is made out of bad stuff. Since matter is bad the God who is pure spirit cannot touch it. He therefore put out a series of aeons or emanations, each one a little more distant from himself, stretching like a kind of ladder between himself and matter. The further the series descended, the further the emanation was from God, the more ignorant of God it was. As the series still further descended, to ignorance there was added hostility; and so at the end of the series there is an aeon, the Demiurge, the World-fashioner, who is utterly ignorant of, and totally hostile to, the true God who is spirit, and by that power the world was created. Creation is essentially evil because it was carried out by an ignorant, hostile, inferior deity working with flawed and imperfect material. Given the premises, it is a perfectly logical explanation of the presence of evil in the world.

The Christian answer is No; creation is not the work of a hostile, bungling, ignorant power; it is the work of the *Logos*, the Word, the Son. Now let us see what this practically means.

Let us again remind ourselves who the *Logos* is – the *Logos* is the perfect expression of the mind of God. In the kindness and the graciousness and the love of Jesus we see God in action. If then the *Logos* is the agent of creation it means that the principle which is in the created world is the same principle as is in Jesus Christ. It means that the God of creation and the God of redemption are one and the same; it means that the love which is in redemption is in creation also.

There are times when only the clinging to that principle prevents the complete collapse of faith. There are times when life seems our enemy. Pain may agonize the body and sorrow may bring anguish to the mind; wave upon wave of disaster may engulf life. But, if we believe that the principle of creation and the principle of redemption are the same, then we can be absolutely sure that life is out to make us and not to break us, that 'it means intensely and means good', and we too can say: 'God, thou art love, I build my faith on that.' The idea of the Christ of creation is not merely a cosmological speculation; it is also many a time the stay and the refuge of the broken heart.

3. Jesus goes on to tell us *what Jesus became*. 'The Word became flesh' (John 1.14). To John's readers this must have seemed the most startling statement in the whole Gospel. Augustine, who was a very great classical scholar, said in his *Confessions* (6.9) that he had found in the great classical thinkers some kind of parallel for everything in the Gospels except this one statement, 'The Word became flesh.'

For a Gnostic the body is clearly essentially evil, for the body is matter. But apart from Gnosticism there was in Graeco-Roman thought a profound belief that the one thing to be desired was to be rid of the body. *Sōma sēma* ran the Orphic jingle, 'The body is a tomb'. The body, said Philolaus, is a house of detention in which the soul is imprisoned to expiate its sin. Philosophy, said Plato, is the study of dying; to have a body is to be contaminated with evil; the body is a prison-house and death the only release (*Phaedo* 64-67). Epictetus described himself as a poor soul shackled to a corpse (*Fragment* 23). Seneca spoke of the detestable habitation of the body (*Letters* 92.110). That God could in any sense take upon himself a body was to the Greek incredible. We shall later, when we are studying John's letters, see how this conception drifted into the Church and threatened disastrous consequences to the Christian faith. At the moment it is enough to say this, no Christian can ever despise the body, for God himself took this human flesh upon him.

4. John goes on to say *what Jesus gives*. As John sees it, Jesus gives three things.

(*a*) Jesus gives *life*. This is the statement which is the beginning the middle and the end of the Fourth Gospel. The Gospel begins: 'In him was life' (1.4). In the middle Jesus claims that he came to give life and life more abundant (10.10). The Gospel ends with the statement that it was written to enable men to believe in Jesus Christ and to have life through his name (20.31).

This life is *eternal life*. The word for *eternal* is *aiōnios*, which means far more than life which lasts indefinitely, for quite clearly mere prolongation of life might be the supreme punishment and curse. *Aiōnios* in Greek is a word of mystery; there is only one person to whom it may properly be applied and that one person is God. Eternal life is nothing other than the life of God. The gift of Jesus Christ here and now is a foretaste of the life divine.

(*b*) Jesus gives *light*. He is the true light (1.9). The word for *true* is here *alēthinos*, which means *real* or *genuine*, as opposed to that which is substitute and counterfeit. Jesus is the real light. Other lights flicker and die, mislead and seduce; he alone is the light which is real and which leads to reality.

(*c*) Jesus gives the *new birth* (1.12, 13). The change he works is so radical that it cannot be called anything less than a new birth. In him life begins again, and in him the coward becomes the hero, the sinner becomes the saint, and the man of the world becomes the man of God.

5. Lastly, John tells us *what Jesus suffered*. He came to his own world and the world did not know him; he came to his own home and his people refused to receive him (1.10, 11). Here is the tragedy of the glory offered, and the glory refused.

To John the supreme fact about Jesus is that Jesus is the perfect expression of the mind of God. We can be quite certain that God cares and God shares. Of whom, then, shall we be afraid?

4
Paul

The Gospel of Faith

Paul's problem was the problem of every man who is aware that there is a God; his problem was how to get into a right relationship with God, how to escape from a situation dominated by distance, fear, estrangement, frustration into a relationship enriched by intimacy, friendship, confidence and trust. In one of his novels, H. G. Wells has a picture of a big business man who was so tensed and strained with the pace of living that he was in danger of complete collapse. His doctor told him that his one hope of sanity and balance lay in finding some kind of fellowship with God. 'What?' the man said. 'That up there having fellowship with me? I would as soon think of cooling my throat with the milky way or shaking hands with the stars!' To him fellowship with God seemed an impossible dream.

Paul was a devout Jew and he had already reached the highest levels of his ancestral religion (Philippians 3.4, 5; II Corinthians 11.21, 22). What was that way towards fellowship upon which Paul had struggled only to find that it was a dead end? It was the way of obedience to the Law.

We shall never go far in the study of Jewish religion without coming upon the idea of the *covenant*. The Jews believed, and rightly, that as a nation they were in a special relationship with God. That relationship they called the covenant relationship. A covenant is not a bargain, an agreement, a treaty, a contract, for in all such relationships the two parties come together on equal terms and with equal rights. The covenant was a relationship in which the whole initiative lay with God. God on his own initiative, not because of any merits of Israel, out of his own free grace, had come to Israel with the special offer that they would be his people and he would be their God. But the covenant was not without its conditions; the privilege was not without its responsibilities. The condition was that Israel must accept and obey the Law which God gave them. In Exodus 24.3-8 we have a vivid picture of the people entering into this relationship with God. The culmination of the initiation came when Moses took the book of the Law and read it to the people and the people said: 'All that the Lord has spoken we will do, and we will be obedient' (Exodus 24.7).

The immediate consequence of this was that the Law became the greatest reality in the religion of Israel. It came to be regarded as divine and pre-existent, as absolutely final and complete, as that part of Scripture to which the rest of Scripture was no more than commentary and addendum. It came to be traced back until it could be said that Adam was circumcised and kept the Sabbath and that Abraham and all the patriarchs kept the Law, as it were, by anticipation. It came even to be said that God himself studied the Law.

It has to be carefully remembered that the expression the Law has three meanings. First, it can mean the Ten Commandments, which are the Law *par excellence*. Second, it can mean the Pentateuch, the first five books of the OT which contain both the moral and the ceremonial law. Third, it can mean the Oral Law. In the beginning the Law had consisted of a series of great principles, such as, 'Remember the Sabbath day to keep it holy.' The Scribes and Rabbis throughout the ages had taken these great principles and had worked them out in the greatest possible detail. For instance, the Law said that a burden must not be carried on the Sabbath; the Scribes spent pages and chapters defining what a burden was, until it came to be argued whether a man was carrying a burden if he wore his dentures or a wooden leg on the Sabbath. According to the ceremonial law the hands must be washed at certain times; the Scribes spent hours defining just how much water must be used, just what the correct actions were. The Oral or Scribal Law took the great principles of the Law and made them into an infinity of rules and regulations. Law had become legalism. And it must always be remembered that it was not the great principles of the divine Law which Paul was against; it was the legalism of the endless details of the Scribal Law.

Clearly, the other side of the Law is obedience. The Jews were the people who had taken upon themselves 'the yoke of the Law' (*Sayings of the Fathers* 3.8). Law is irrelevant unless it is meticulously obeyed. Two facts are to be noted about this obedience.

First, for the devout Jew this obedience was a joy and a glory. 'The Law is my delight,' said the Psalmist. 'Oh, how I love thy law!' (Psalm 119.77, 97). The law was not the yoke of slavery; it was the yoke which a lover takes upon himself when he dedicates himself in devotion to obey the least command of his beloved.

Second, it is nonetheless true that this view of religion produces, or is liable to produce, the most serious consequences. If a relationship is dependent on the obedience to law, especially if that law is conceived of in terms of rules and regulations, the idea of merit inevitably enters in. The man who obeys the regulations acquires a credit balance; the man who fails to do so acquires a debit balance. In this relationship a man can work his passage. It is possible to speak of those who have been justified in their keeping of the Law (II Baruch 51.3, 4). Hezekiah the good king trusted in his works (II Baruch 63.3).

There is even a treasury of works. The righteous have with God a store of works preserved in treasuries (II Baruch 14.12). The good man has a treasure of works laid up with the Most High (II Esdras 7.77).

This situation can result in one of two things which depend largely on the temperament of the person involved. It can result in spiritual pride. The more detailed the Law became, the more the opportunities arose to score credits and to acquire merit. And it became possible for a man of a certain type of mind to congratulate himself on the meticulous performance of the regulations of the Law, and even to think that he had succeeded in putting God in his debt. Hence pride and self-righteousness arise.

The second result is the precise opposite of this. A man could become agonized and tortured and frustrated and defeated when he allowed himself to think of the sinner's attempt to satisfy the sinless One, of humanity's hopeless struggle to set itself right with deity. Clearly, this is a struggle doomed to defeat, and can result only in a terrible estrangement, conscious for ever of being in default to God and under the judgment of God.

It was the second situation in which Paul found himself. No human being had ever striven harder and succeeded better in keeping the Law. As far as the righteousness which was in the Law was concerned he was blameless (Philippians 3.6). But the harder he strove the further he became from God. 'No human being', he said, 'will be justified in God's sight by works of the Law' (Romans 3.20; Galatians 3.11). 'A man is not justified by works of the Law' (Galatians 2.16). Paul knew, because Paul had tried it.

And yet the curious thing is that to the end of the day Paul never discarded the Law, although when he speaks of the Law in this sense it is not the Scribal Law, but the great principles of the Divine Law which he has in mind. 'Do we then overthrow the Law by this faith? By no means! On the contrary, we uphold the Law' (Romans 3.31). The commandment is holy, just and good (Romans 7.12). What then is the use of the Law and the place of the Law in the new scheme of things?

1. Quite clearly, the Law defines sin. If it had not been for the Law, Paul would not have known what sin was (Romans 7.7). Where there is no Law, there can be no charge of sin (Romans 5.13). Through the Law comes the knowledge of sin (Romans 3.20). To take a very simple example, in the early stages of the OT polygamy was practised, but it was not yet wrong, for the divine law forbidding it was not yet known to men. There is a sense, a quite neutral sense, in which the Law creates sin. The Law came in to increase the trespass (Romans 5.20). To take an analogy, for long enough it may be quite legal to drive along a road in either direction; a regulation is passed making that road a one-way road; and immediately a new 'sin', the sin of driving in the wrong direction, is thereby created. Certainly the Law is necessary to define sin.

2. But there is another sense in which the Law creates sin. Sin found its opportunity through the commandment (Romans 7.7-11). It is a bitter fact of human experience that it often happens that no sooner is a thing forbidden than it becomes desirable. The very fact that it was forbidden to eat of the tree in the garden made Adam and Eve wish to eat it. The grass on the other side of the fence is always most succulent. The paradox and tragedy of the Law is that it creates a desire for that which it forbids. Sin works in a man through that which is in itself good. So there arises a situation in which a man is consumed with desire for that which he knows is wrong and which one part of him does not wish to do, and a barrier is set up, stopping him doing what he really wishes to do. The Law has made him a split personality and a walking civil war (Romans 7.13-25).

3. Is then the Law totally wrong and useless? There are two things the Law can do.

(a) The Law shuts a man up under sin (Galatians 3.23). It compels him to see the slavery in which he lives. It compels him to fulfil the old Greek adage and to know himself. In this the Law is essential for the first step to freedom is to realize that we are slaves.

(b) The Law does more than that. It is, as the AV has it, our *schoolmaster* to lead us to Christ (Galatians 3.24). The word is *paidagōgos*, and *schoolmaster* is not a good translation. The RSV has *custodian*; Weymouth, *tutor slave*; Moffatt has it that the Law *held us wards in discipline*; Kingsley Williams has *the slave that disciplined us*; the NEB, *a kind of tutor in charge of us*; Phillips has it that the Law is *a strict governess*. The fact is that the *paidagōgos* had nothing to do with a boy's technical education. He did teach the boy manners and morals; and he did every day conduct the boy to the door of the schoolroom, and leave him there. He took him to school, but he never himself entered the school. He, as it were, handed him over and delivered him to the one who could teach him. So then the Law brings us to the door of Christ and leaves us there.

What does this mean? It can only mean that the Law drives us to complete despair. It shows us the good; it leaves us helpless to do it; it even wakens the desire to sin. Life is defeated and frustrated, and there is nothing left to do but to come to Jesus Christ and accept what he has to give. The Law can take us so far, but only Jesus Christ can take us the whole way to God. When then is to be put in the place of Law?

Not we have arrived at the great Pauline conception of *faith*. Faith is a kaleidoscopic word, and we can only take the most summary view of it here.

1. Faith is *loyalty*. The faith of the Christians at Rome is proclaimed throughout the world (Romans 1.8). The faith of

the Colossians and the Thessalonians is dear to Paul (Colossians 1.4; I Thessalonians 3.5). The Corinthians are to stand fast in the faith (I Corinthians 16.13). Man's faithlessness is contrasted with God's faith, God's reliability, God's loyalty to himself and to his promises and to his people (Romans 3.3). Faith is that loyalty which is the foundation stone of life and of religion.

2. Faith is a man's *religion*. The Christians were amazed to find Paul preaching the faith he had once sought to obliterate (Galatians 1.23). The man who is weak in the faith must not be immediately introduced to debates about doubtful questions (Romans 14.1). We speak of the Christian faith in the sense of the Christian religion.

3. Faith is a *creed*, that in which a man believes and by which he is prepared to stand. There is one Lord, one faith, one baptism (Ephesians 4.5).

4. Faith *comes from hearing*. It is the result of listening in the right way to a message which is a challenge and a rebuke and an offer (Romans 10.17; Galatians 3.2).

5. It is now that we come to the distinctively Pauline sense of faith. Faith is *committal to an adventure*. We walk by faith and not by sight (II Corinthians 5.7). It is launching out into the deep, accepting the plunge into the unknown, 'betting your life that there is a God'. It is venturing for the name of Christ.

6. Faith is the *trustful acceptance of an offer*. It is by faith that the expiation of Christ must be received (Romans 3.25). It is the committal of all life in time and in eternity to the trust that the offer and promises of God in Christ Jesus are true. It is casting oneself without reservation on God in the complete confidence that he means what he says in Christ.

7. Faith is the *willingness to admit one's own helplessness*. This is the essence of the contrast between faith and works (Romans 3.28; 9.32). The man who believes in works thinks consciously or unconsciously that he can do something to save

himself, something to put himself right with God; faith means the acceptance of the fact that a man can do nothing except humbly and trustfully accept what God offers him. Faith is the realization that man can only take.

8. Faith can only work *through love and must change the frustration of life into the joy of life* (Galatians 5.6; Ephesians 6.23; II Thessalonians 1.3; Philippians 1.25). It is neither the arid intellectualism which thinks only of the mind nor the gloom which is obsessed with sin. It is the kindled heart and the joyous spirit whose confidence is not in self but in God.

For Paul faith is exemplified in Abraham (Romans 4; Galatians 3.6-18). Abraham was not justified by works of the Law, nor by circumcision, because he lived long before the Law was given, and his circumcision followed and did not precede the establishment of his relationship with God. Faith in Abraham was simply the willingness to take God at his word even if the word seemed impossible. It seemed humanly impossible that a man of a hundred years of age with a wife as old should have a child, yet Abraham believed that what God promised God would do. Abraham was the man who took God at his word, and that is faith.

Paul expresses this new relationship between God and man in a series of metaphors.

1. There is the metaphor from *slavery* and the idea of *emancipation*. The Christian has been bought with a great price (I Corinthians 6.20; 7.23); God has purchased the Church with the blood of his own One (Acts 20.28). It is for freedom that Christ has set us free (Gal. 5.1).

In the Greek world it was possible for a slave to gain his freedom. He might during any free time he had work for a few coppers. Each time he earned some money he deposited it in the temple of some god. He might well have to go on doing this for many long years. When he had the total purchase price deposited, he took his master to the temple; the priest paid over the money; and then the slave became the property of the god and therefore free of all men. So Paul thinks of Jesus Christ as paying the purchase price, which brings a man into the possession of God, and from that time on a man is no longer the slave of sin but the servant of righteousness (Romans 6.14-23). Thus through the price that Jesus Christ paid a man is liberated and emancipated from sin and becomes the property of God.

2. There is the metaphor from the *family* and the idea of *adoption*. Through Jesus Christ we have received the spirit of sonship or adoption (Romans 8.15; Galatians 4.5, 6; Ephesians 1.5). We have become members of the family of God and can speak of God as Abba, Father.

In the ancient world adoption was common, and in the Roman world it almost literally made a man a new man. All the obligations and debts of his past life were cancelled, and he became as really a son of his adopting father as any flesh and blood son was. He left behind him all the old debts and entered without restriction into all the new privileges.

3. There is the metaphor from *friendship* and the idea of *reconciliation*. We are reconciled to God by the death of his Son (Romans 5.10). God was in Christ reconciling the world to himself (II Corinthians 5.18-20). The verb is *katallassein* and it is the regular Greek verb for effecting a reconciliation between two people who have quarrelled or drifted apart. Through Jesus Christ friendship between man and God is restored. But one thing must be noted – it is always man who is reconciled to God, never God to man. It was not the attitude of God which had to be changed; that was always suffering, waiting, seeking love. It was man's heart which had to be changed so that the rebellion should become obedience and the fear should become trust.

4. There is the metaphor from *sacrifice* and the idea of *propitiation*. God put Jesus Christ forward as an expiation in his

blood (Romans 3.25). We are here in the realm of the covenant again. We have seen that the existence of the covenant relationship depended on the keeping of the Law. Man being sinful, the covenant relationship was bound to be broken. To meet that situation the whole sacrificial system was created. When a man broke the Law, he came with a sacrifice which was the sign and the symbol and the guarantee of his penitence, and thus the relationship was restored. It has to be noted that, whatever may have ultimately been the popular belief, the sacrifice was unavailing without the penitence of which it was the sign.

Sacrifice is therefore the way towards the restoration of the broken relationship between man and God in Jewish thought. So the life and death of Jesus Christ are the price at which man's relationship to God was restored. This sacrifice did not change the attitude of God, for, as we have seen, God never needed to be reconciled to man. The plea is: 'Be reconciled to God' (II Corinthians 5.20). God's wrath never needed to be changed to love, for it was his love that God showed in that while we were yet sinners Christ died for us (Romans 5.8). It was God himself who in the wonder of his love thus reached out in the sufferings and death of his Son to touch the hearts of men.

5. There is the metaphor from the *lawcourts* and the idea of *justification*. It is here we reach the very heart of Paul's own faith, for here we reach the doctrine of Justification by Faith. No man can be justified by works; that Paul knew from bitter experience (Romans 3.20; Galatians 2.16; 3.11). A man is justified by faith and therein finds his peace with God (Romans 3.28; 5.1).

It is unfortunate that here the word *justification* is being used in a non-English and an unusual sense. Usually the verb to justify means to produce reasons why a person was right to act as he did. But when Paul says that God justifies the ungodly

(Romans 4.5) it is clear that he cannot mean that God produces reasons to prove that the sinner was right to act as he did, and is right to be a sinner. In Greek the verb is *dikaioun*. Greek verbs which end in -*oun*, when they describe moral qualities, do not mean to make a man such and such a thing, they mean to treat, reckon, account, regard a man as such and such a thing. So when Paul speaks of God justifying the ungodly, quite simply he means that *God treats the sinner as if he was a good man*. In his amazing love God treats the hell-deserving sinner as a beloved son. The perfect example of Justification by Faith in action is the parable of the prodigal son. The son planned to come back and to ask to be received as a hired servant; he never got the chance to make the request; he is welcomed as a son (Luke 15.11-32). Here indeed is a Gospel. All that we could have expected is condemnation, and lo and behold we meet with welcoming love. The relationship between God and man is completely changed. We can now think of God not as the threatening judge but as the waiting father, and we can come to him in heart-broken penitence but nonetheless in childlike confidence and trust.

If every time we meet the word justification we translate it to come into a right relationship with God, the whole matter becomes clear. No human being can ever enter into a right relationship with God through works of the Law (Romans 3.20). Since through faith we are in a right relationship with God we have peace with him through Jesus Christ (Romans 5.1).

Why *by faith*? Because all this sounds too good to be true, and all that we can do is to make the act of trust which accepts it as true, and which in that trust comes to God. Why *through Jesus Christ*? Because apart from Jesus Christ and without him no man could ever have discovered that God is like this.

The other name for all this is *grace*. Grace is something

which a man can never earn, but which is freely and spontaneously given to him, and which he can only accept. The essence of the Pauline faith is the acceptance of the fact that we cannot save ourselves, but that we can only trustingly and lovingly accept that which God so generously offers.

But the matter cannot be left there. It would be possible to interpret all that we have so far seen as a reason for holding that sin does not matter any more. If God treats the sinner as a good man, why worry about sin any more? If grace is all-important, and if man must stop striving and start receiving, why not simply relax all discipline and let desire have full play? In point of fact this is precisely the argument that Paul had to meet, and we shall meet it again in other parts of the NT. Behind the questions in Romans 6.1 there is a hidden conversation. 'What shall we then say? Are we to continue in sin that grace may abound?' The argument runs like this.

The Questioner: You say that grace can forgive any sin?
Paul: I do.
The Questioner: You say that grace is the greatest and loveliest thing in the world?
Paul: I do.
The Questioner: Then, if that be so, let us go on sinning to our heart's content, for the more we sin the more this tremendous grace receives its opportunity to operate. All that it does is to provide an opportunity for the grace of God.

To that Paul would have returned three answers.

1. What Christianity does is not to supply a man with an excuse comfortably to live the old life; it supplies him with a dynamic for the new life. That new life which comes with baptism is a sharing in the resurrection life of Christ. In it a man

has died to sin and lives to God; he is no longer the slave of sin but the servant of righteousness (Romans 6.3-19). The whole essence of Christianity is not that it makes a man free to sin, but that it makes him free not to sin.

2. If a man takes up that attitude he does not know what love is. The fact that our nearest and dearest love us and will love us and will forgive us no matter what we do is not a reason for doing the things which will break their hearts; so far from that it lays upon us the responsibility of for ever seeking to deserve that love. To know that we are loved, and to know that love will forgive, is not a reason for licence; it is the obligation to nobility.

3. The Pauline idea of justification is incomplete without the accompanying idea of *sanctification*. When the Christian is freed from sin and becomes the slave of God, the return he receives is sanctification (Romans 6.22). The sanctification of the Christian is the will of God (I Thessalonians 4.3). It is Paul's prayer for the Thessalonians that the God of peace may sanctify his people wholly (I Thessalonians 5.23). Christians are chosen for salvation through sanctification by the Spirit (II Thessalonians 2.13).

What is this sanctification? The word for *sanctification* is *hagiasmos*; Greek nouns which end in *-asmos* signify not an act but a process; and sanctification is *the road to holiness*, and it is precisely that road that the Christian must for ever walk. Take an analogy. Suppose there is a locomotive which must pull a train from London to Glasgow. It is facing in the wrong direction. It is taken to the turn-table and turned round. But then after that it must begin on the long journey to its appointed destination. Conversion, justification, the moment when we turn round and face God in the new relationship, instead of running away from him, is like the turning on the turn-table. Sanctification is like the long road which has to be made to the journey's end. Paul would certainly have said that a man is not saved *by* works; but he would equally have said that a man is saved *for* works. And unless sanctification follows justification, unless a moral change accompanies the new relationship to God, a man's Christianity is sadly incomplete.

But there is this one difference. The motive power is not now law but love. The constraint now is the love of Christ (II Corinthians 5.14). The dynamic is not now fear, but devotion to the Savior who loved us and gave himself for us. Life has become a response to love, and has laid upon it the awesome responsibility of being loved.

When all this happens, then life is *in Christ*, a phrase which occurs in Paul's letters more than eighty times. It has been said that the only possible analogy to this phrase is in our relationship to the air which surrounds us. Unless we are in the air, and unless the air is in us, we die. And unless the Christian is in Christ and Christ in the Christian the spiritual life dies. Christ is the very atmosphere in which the Christian lives and moves and has his being, the standard by which he judges all things, the voice for which he continually listens, the presence who is always and for ever with him in life and in death.

5

The Letter to the Hebrews

The Gospel of the Approach to God

It may well be said that the whole of the Letter to the Hebrews
is written on one text: 'Let us draw near' (10.22). Its central
idea is the new and free approach to God which has become
possible through Jesus Christ.

The writer to the Hebrews wrote out of a double
background. The thinkers and the seekers from the two
backgrounds would have used different language and different
categories of thought, but fundamentally they would have been
saying the same thing and searching for the same thing.

The writer to the Hebrews wrote out of *a Greek background*.
It was Plato who gave the world the conception of forms or
ideas. For him the unseen world was the real world. In it there
were laid up the forms, the ideas, the perfect archetypes and
patterns of which everything in this world is a pale and
imperfect copy. To put it at its very simplest, there is in the
unseen world a perfect idea of a chair of which all man-made
chairs are imperfect copies. This world of space and time is not
the real world; the things which we can see and touch and
handle are not the real things. The real world is the invisible
world beyond. Philo believed that God created the unseen
world first with all its perfect patterns, and then created the
visible world as a copy of the unseen (*Concerning the Creator of
the World* 16). Seneca explains to Lucilius that the ideas of
which Plato spoke were 'what all visible things were created

from and what formed the pattern for all things' (*Letters* 57.18, 19). In the Letter to the Hebrews there is a direct echo of this when the writer speaks of the Temple in Jerusalem as being 'a copy and shadow of the heavenly sanctuary', and when he recalls how Moses was instructed to make everything according to the pattern shown to him on the heavenly mount (8.5). For the Greek, then, the search was for access to reality in the invisible world beyond.

The writer to the Hebrews wrote out of a *Hebrew* background. There was one essential difference between Greek and Hebrew thought. The Greek searched for *truth*; the Hebrew searched for *God*. The Greek searched for knowledge; the Hebrew searched for the living God. For the Greek at the end of the search there was a truth; for the Hebrew at the end of the search there was a person. The Hebrew would always say, not: 'I know *what* I have believed', but 'I know *whom* I have believed' (II Timothy 1.12). Further, when we were studying the Fourth Gospel, we have already seen that the Greek would regard the discovery of truth of God as impossible so long as a man was shackled and imprisoned in the body. Even the Wisdom literature of the Jews has an echo of this line of thought. 'The corruptible body', says the Sage, 'presses down upon the soul, and the earthly tabernacle weighs down the mind that muses upon many things' (Wisdom 9.15). But the true Hebrew would certainly hold that a man can know God here and now.

So then the Hebrew sought for God; and therein precisely lies his problem. God to the Hebrew was *holy, kadosh* in Hebrew, *hagios* in Greek; and the basic meaning of this word is *separate, different, other*. God, as modern theology was later to express it, is the Wholly Other. Not only did the Hebrew think of God as wholly other; he also regarded it as dangerous and even deadly to seek to approach that white blaze of purity in which God lives.

Moses heard God say: 'You cannot see my face; for man shall not see me and live' (Exodus 33.20). After the incident at Peniel it was Jacob's astonished exclamation: 'I have seen God face to face and yet my life is preserved' (Genesis 32.30). When Moses came down from the mount the people exclaimed in astonishment: 'We have this day seen God speak with man and man still live' (Deuteronomy 5.24). When Manoah discovered who his heavenly visitor had been, he said to his wife in terror: 'We shall surely die because we have seen God' (Judges 13.22). When Gideon knew to whom he had been speaking, and when terror gripped him, the voice of God calmed him: 'Peace be to you; do not fear, you shall not die' (Judges 6.22, 23). Into the Holy of Holies in the Temple no man but the High Priest might go, and he only on the Day of Atonement (Leviticus 16); and even in his case the regulations laid it down that he must not linger too long in that holiness, 'lest he put Israel in terror'.

Here then was the situation. The Greek was seeking access to that elusive reality which he could only find when he had sloughed off the body; the Jew was seeking access to the God who was the Holy One and the Wholly Other. The argument of the writer to the Hebrews is that Jesus is the only one in whom there is free and open access to reality and to God. To this end the writer to the Hebrews describes Jesus under five great terms.

1. Jesus is the *archēgos* of our faith (12.2). The AV renders *author*, with *beginner* in the margin; the RV, *author*, with *captain* in the margin; the RSV and Moffatt, *pioneer*; Weymouth, *Prince Leader*; Kingsley Williams, *leader*; Knox, *origin*; Phillips, *source*; Wuest, *originator*. The NEB speaks of Jesus *on whom our faith depends from start to finish*.

Obviously, the word is not easy to render. It has two lines of meaning. First, it does mean a prince, a leader, a commander. Second, its more characteristic meaning is that of a beginner of something which still exists. Thus it can mean the founder of a city or a family or a school of philosophy, the one who blazes the trail for others to follow in his footsteps. Someone has used the analogy from a shipwreck. If a ship is wrecked and some gallant man swims ashore with a rope along which others can follow in safety, that man is the *archēgos*. He went first to make it possible for others to follow. So Jesus is the pioneer who blazes the way into the presence of God that we may follow.

2. Jesus is the *prodromos* (6.20). *Prodromos* is a military word, and the *prodromoi* were the scouts who went on ahead to see that it was safe for the main body to follow. It has been said that the word was used to describe the pilot boat which sailed in front of the larger vessels, as they entered the harbor of Alexandria, to show them where the right channel was. Here we have the same idea again. Jesus goes first for us to follow.

3. Central to the thought of the writer to the Hebrews is the idea of the *covenant*, and in this connection he uses two other terms about Jesus. Jesus is the *egguos*, the surety or guarantor of a better covenant (7.22), and he is the *mesitēs*, the mediator of the new covenant (8.6; 9.15; 12.24).

The covenant, as we have seen, was a relationship between God and Israel, in which God in his free, spontaneous grace had chosen Israel to be his people, and had offered himself as their God. The maintenance of the covenant was dependent on the keeping of the Law (Exodus 24.3-8). The sacrificial system was devised to restore the relationship when man's disobedience had broken it. Quite clearly, for all its greatness this covenant is very imperfect.

(*a*) The Law is bound to be broken. Since man is a sinner, he cannot fully keep and obey the Divine Law. To make the covenant dependent on that is to make it dependent on an impossibility.

(*b*) The priests are doubly imperfect. First, the priest, being himself a sinner, must first offer sacrifice for his own sins (7.27).

A sinner cannot really be the means of atoning for sin. Second, the priests of the old covenant are subject to death. Being mortal men, they are born and die, and come and go with no permanency (7.23).

(*c*) The sacrifices of the old covenant are clearly ineffective, because day in and day out they have to be made over and over again. Whatever temporary effect they may have, they have no permanent effect on the situation created by sin (10.1-3).

(*d*) In any event the sacrifice of animals is unavailing because what God desires is the sacrifice a life dedicated in loving obedience to his will (10.5-10).

The old covenant is a shadow and a copy of reality, but it is not the real thing. But there is nothing surprising in this, for the OT itself spoke of a new covenant: 'Behold the days are coming, says the Lord, when I will make a new covenant with the house of Israel and the house of Judah, not like the covenant which I made with their fathers when I took them by the hand to bring them out of the land of Egypt, my covenant which they broke, though I was their husband, says the Lord. But this is the covenant which I will make with the house of Israel after those days, says the Lord; I will put my law within them, and I will write it upon their hearts; and I will be their God, and they shall be my people. And no longer shall each man teach his neighbor and each his brother, saying, Know the Lord, for they shall all know me, from the least even unto the greatest, says the Lord; for I will forgive their iniquity, and I will remember their sin no more' (Jeremiah 31.31-34). The very fact that a new covenant is promised shows that the old covenant is obsolete, outdated, and passing away (8.13). And it is to be noted that this new covenant knows nothing of an externally imposed law written in a book; its law is written on the heart; nor does it know anything of sacrifice; the need for sacrifice no longer exists.

It is the claim of the writer to the Hebrews that that new

covenant has come in Jesus Christ. Of that new covenant Jesus is the *egguos*, the sponsor, the guarantor. Of that new covenant he is the *mesitēs*. *Mesos* means *in the middle*; and a *mesitēs* was a *middleman*, who stood between two people who were estranged and drew them together again.

(*e*) Let us now see more closely the relationship of Jesus to this new covenant. The new covenant needs *a perfect sacrifice*. Jesus had made that. Once and for all in offering himself he has made a sacrifice that never needs to be repeated (7.27). The new covenant needs *a perfect priest*. Jesus is that. Firstly, he is completely identified with the men he came to save. A priest must be such that he can deal gently with the ignorant and the wayward, since he himself is beset with weakness (5.1, 2). 'We have not a high priest who is unable to sympathize with our weaknesses, but one who in every respect has been tempted as we are, yet without sinning' (4.15). No writer in the NT has a deeper sense of the identification of Jesus with the human situation (2.14; 5.7, 8; 12.2, 3; 13.12). Secondly, the perfect priest cannot take his office upon himself; he must be divinely appointed (5.1). And it is here that the writer to the Hebrews makes his personal and unique contribution to the understanding of Jesus, for he shows us Jesus as *the High Priest according to the* order of Melchizedek. His picture is wrought out in two passages, which should be carefully studied, 5.1-10 and the whole of chapter 7.

He founds his argument on two OT passages to which he brings all the skill of expert Jewish rabbinic exegesis.

The Lord hath sworn and will not change his mind, 'You are a priest for ever after the order of Melchizedek'.

(Psalm 110.4)

After his return from the defeat of Chedorlaomer, and the kings who were with him, the king of Sodom went out to meet him

(Abraham) at the Valley of Shaveh (that is, the King's Valley). And
Melchizedek king of Salem brought him bread and wine; he was
the priest of God Most High. And he blessed him and said:

Blessed be Abraham by God Most High,
    maker of heaven and earth;
and blessed be God Most High,
    who has delivered your enemies into your hand!

(Genesis 14.17-20)

Here a new and unknown priesthood is described, a priesthood
which, as the writer to the Hebrews saw it, was the forecast and
the symbol of the priesthood of Jesus Christ. Let us then follow
the argument of the writer to the Hebrews in chapter 7 to see
what these passages say to him about the priesthood of Jesus
Christ and its superiority to the existing levitical priesthood.

The priesthood of Jesus Christ is a *royal* priesthood, for
Melchizedek was a king. It is a *righteous* priesthood, for
Melchizedek means king of *righteousness*. It is a *peaceful*
priesthood, for Melchizedek was king of Salem, and Salem is
taken to mean *peace*. The levitical priesthood was entirely
dependent on descent from Aaron, and such descent had to be
proved and guaranteed; but there is no mention of any
genealogy, of any father or mother of Melchizedek; the new
priesthood therefore depends on *personal power and quality*
and not on any family tree. There is no mention whatever of
either the birth or the death of Melchizedek; he appears as
timeless; therefore the new priesthood is *eternal*, without
beginning or end, beginning before time began and unending
when time ends.

Now follow a series of arguments to prove the superiority of
the new priesthood. The superior always blesses the inferior.
Therefore, since Melchizedek blessed Abraham, he is the
superior of Abraham, who is no less than the founder of the

nation of Israel. Ordinarily it is the Levites who receive tithes, and they do so because the Law entitles them to do so. But Melchizedek was no Levite and yet he received tithes, not because the Law assigned them to him, but as a perfect personal right. Further, the Levites tithe their brethren, but Melchizedek tithed Abraham who was a total stranger to him. Still further, Levi himself paid tithes to Melchizedek, because, although yet unborn, he might be said to be in the body of his great-grandfather Abraham. Every stone in the edifice shows the superiority of the priesthood according to the order of Melchizedek to the levitical priesthood.

Still further, the priesthood according to the order of Melchizedek is confirmed by nothing less than the oath of God (Psalm 110.4), which makes it far greater than the levitical priesthood. The very mention of the priesthood according to the order of Melchizedek demonstrates the inferiority of the levitical priesthood, for, if the levitical priesthood had been adequate and effective, no other priesthood would ever have been mentioned. And this new priesthood is a complete revolution. The priests came from the tribe of *Levi*, but Jesus came from the tribe of *Judah*, from which no priests ever came; and this is the proof, not only of a new kind of priesthood, but of the total abrogation of the old law. Finally, two facts are brought forward which we have already noted. The new priest need make no sacrifice for his own sin for he is sinless, and the sacrifice he made never needs to be repeated but is for ever and for ever effective and availing.

Such is the picture of the priesthood according to the order of Melchizedek, the new priesthood which put the old priesthood for ever out of date.

There remains one thing to note. The writer to the Hebrews had an almost unique sense of the total adequacy of the work of Jesus Christ. It stretches back into the past, for it redeems men from transgressions committed under the old covenant (9.15). It reaches forward into the future, for the work of Jesus Christ as high priest is never ended. Even in the heavenly places he carries on his priestly work, for we have a high priest who has passed through the heavens (4.14). He appears in the presence of God on our behalf (9.24). He continues a priest for ever (7.3). He is able for all time to save those who draw near to God through him, since he always lives to make intercession for them (7.25). Here is a picture of Jesus Christ saving in past time, saving in present time, and saving for ever and for ever. And in this picture and behind it there is something even more far-reaching. Its real meaning is that the life and the death and the Cross of Christ are not, as it were, parts of some isolated incident. The incarnation and the crucifixion are not, as it were, emergency measures. This was not done because everything else had been tried and failed. The life and death of Jesus are not simply events in time; they are windows into the eternal heart of God, whereby we see the suffering and redeeming love of God which has been suffering and redeeming since the beginning of time and will be beyond the end of time. In Jesus Christ we see God, not as God for a moment became, but as God for ever was, for ever is, and for ever will be.

The Latin Word for priest is *pontifex*, which literally means *a bridge-builder*, and for the writer to the Hebrews the Gospel's essence is that Jesus Christ is for men the bridge into the presence of God. 'Therefore, brethren, since we have confidence to enter the sanctuary by the blood of Jesus, by the new and living way which he opened for us through the curtain, that is, through his flesh, and since we have a great high priest over the house of God, *let us draw near* with a true heart in full assurance of faith' (10.19-22).

6
James

The Gospel of Christian Action

The Letter of James has always had a kind of question mark against it. Eusebius, the great Church historian, made in the fourth century an investigation of what might be called the status of the books which the Church used, and as a result classified them as those which were universally accepted and those which were disputed. Amongst the disputed he lists James. 'It is to be observed that it is disputed; at least, not many of the ancients have mentioned it.' He refers to 'the so-called Letter of James' as being among the disputed writings, 'which nevertheless are recognized by many' (*The Ecclesiastical History* 2.23.46; 3.25.3). Jerome, the great Latin scholar who in the fifth century was responsible for the Latin translation of the Bible known as the Vulgate, in his brief biography of James, says: 'James wrote a single Letter ... and even this is claimed by some to have been published by someone else under his name, and gradually, as time went on, to have gained authority' (*Lives of Illustrious Men* 2). The Letter of James was not even translated into Syriac until the middle of the fifth century AD. It is not that the early Church questioned the *value* of the Letter of James, but it did question its *authorship*.

Doubtless all such criticisms would have had very little effect on the later acceptance of the Letter; but what really did affect the status of James was Luther's series of adverse verdicts upon it. Luther indicated the inferior value he set on four books of the

NT by the very way in which he printed the index page of his New Testament. He put Hebrews, James, Jude and the Revelation into a little group by themselves, separated from the others by a space, and, unlike the others, unnumbered. This printing lay-out was followed in the English versions of Tyndale (1525), Coverdale (1535), Matthew (1537) and Taverner (1539). The first English Bible to print the books of the NT in their present order, which is the order of the Vulgate, was the Great Bible (1539), which was followed by the Bishops' Bible (1568), and by the Authorized Version (1611).

But Luther did more than this. He repeatedly in so many words attacked the Letter of James. He wrote in *The Preface to the New Testament*:

> In sum: the Gospel and the First Epistle of John, St Paul's Epistles, especially those to the Romans, Galatians and Ephesians: and St Peter's first Epistle, are the books which show Christ to you. They teach everything you need to know for your salvation, even if you were never to see or hear any other teaching. In comparison with these the Epistle of James is an epistle full of straw (*eyn rechte stroorn epistel*), because it contains nothing evangelical.

(The reference to 'straw' is from I Corinthians 3.12). He developed this attack in *The Preface to the Epistles of St James and St Jude*. James is quite in error when he represents Abraham as being justified by works. He has nothing to say of the Passion, the Resurrection, the Spirit of Christ. He mentions Christ only twice. Luther then goes on to give his own principle for the evaluation of any book:

> The true touchstone for testing any book is to discover whether it emphasizes the prominence of Christ or not. ... What does not teach Christ is not apostolic, not even if taught by Peter or Paul.

On the other hand what does preach Christ is apostolic, even if
Judas, Annas, Pilate or Herod does it.

This test James does not fulfil. 'I', says Luther, 'therefore refuse
him a place among the writers of the true canon of my Bible.'
Again in 1527 we find him saying that James 'was neither
written by an apostle, nor has it the true apostolic ring, nor does
it agree with pure doctrine'. Philip Melanchthon thought that it
was quite possible to harmonize the teaching of James and the
teaching of Paul. But in the *Table-talk* Luther is quoted as
saying: '"Faith justifies," and "Faith does not justify" are plain
contradictions. Whoever can reconcile them, on him will I put
my cap, and allow him to call me a fool.' It is quite clear that a
book subjected to attacks like this from a man like Luther begins
with a handicap, although Calvin was perfectly right when he
said that he saw nothing in James to criticize, because it was
quite unreasonable to expect every man to present the argument
for Christianity and Christ in exactly the same way.

When we turn to examine the teaching of the Letter of
James, we are immediately confronted with a problem. It is
almost impossible to make a connected analysis and scheme of
it. In many ways it is easily the most contemporary book in the
NT. It might have been written yesterday, and there is hardly a
sentence in it which does not speak vividly and directly to today.
But it has this characteristic of disconnectedness. That is so
because James is not really a letter; it is rather a sermon. It may
indeed well have been an actual sermon of James the brother of
our Lord, which someone took down, and translated, and
issued to the Church at large. The deliberate characteristic of
Jewish preaching was disconnectedness. The Jewish Rabbis
declared that the preacher must not linger long on any subject,
lest he lose the interest of his audience; he must move quickly
from one matter to another. Hence one of the Jewish words for

preaching is *charaz* which means *stringing beads together*. So E. J. Goodspeed says of James: 'James is full of gems of religious thought. The question is: How are they related? The work has been compared to a chain, each link related to the one before it and the one after it. Others have compared its contents to beads on a string. ... Perhaps James is not so much a chain of thought, or beads on a string, as it is just a handful of pearls, dropped one by one into the hearer's mind.' This is simply to say that James is a typical Jewish sermon, cast in the form of a letter for the whole Church to read.

The people to whom James wrote were living in a world where it was not easy to be a Christian. They were involved in many a trial (1.2). The trials were not the trials of persecution, which, agonizing though they may be, have nonetheless a certain dramatic, romantic and heroic quality about them. The trials were the trials of men and women who were trying to live the Christian life of mercy, meekness and humility in the midst of an aggressive, self-assertive, competitive and ostentatious society, in which wealth was the touchstone of success. They were confronted with the task of being Christian in a world which was thoroughly worldly. Just because of this there were certain vices and dangers which threatened the life of the Christian in a very special way.

(*a*) There was a danger which threatened their church life, the danger of what the AV calls *respect of person*. The RSV calls it *partiality*, and the NEB, putting it into contemporary language, calls it plainly *snobbery*. In 2.1-7 there is vividly portrayed what could happen in the Church of those days. When a rich man entered the church he was treated with almost fawning attention, and when a poor man entered, he was treated with complete disregard or open and active contempt. A situation like that was almost bound to arise in circumstances in which it was something of an event for anyone of any social standing to become a Christian (I Corinthians 1.26). James is quite certain that there are no distinguished visitors and no very important persons within the fellowship of the Church.

There may well be a further echo of this in James's injunction: 'Let not many of you become teachers, my brethren' (3.1). It is not improbable that there were too many who sought the prominence and the publicity and the prestige which a preacher and a teacher might enjoy. James was sure that, whenever social or intellectual snobbery enters the Church, the Church ceases to be a fellowship and becomes no more than a copy of the competitive society which is the world.

(*b*) There was a danger which threatened their business life. They were apt to make plans in which God was left out of the reckoning (4.13-17). They formed their schemes and their plans as if they were masters of time; it never struck them to say, 'God willing'. In their absorption in the art of making money, they had forgotten God.

(*c*) There was a danger which threatened their personal life. They were apt to set themselves up as critics and judges of others, forgetting that the function of judgment belongs to God (4.11, 12). He who sets himself up as a judge of his fellow-men usurps that prerogative which belongs to God.

(*d*) To James the possession of riches came very near to being a sin. There is an Amos-like quality in his denunciation of the rich. Riches are a perishing commodity, as evanescent as the flower doomed to wither in the heat of the sun (1.10, 11). The rich oppress the poor, and drag him into court for debt (2.6, 7). If the rich realized the doom which was inevitably coming upon them, they would be in mourning and lamentation. Their wealth is rotten and rusted because it has been gained at the cost of cheating the laboring man of his wages and killing the righteous man (5.1-6). It would be difficult for James to believe that great wealth was ever honestly attained.

(*e*) At the back of all this is the passion in the heart of man (4.1-6). It is this passion of covetousness and desire which drives a man to false ambition and to crime, which sets men at war one with another, and which vitiates even prayer by making prayer selfish. Let them humbly submit to God and courageously resist the devil. Let them acquire real cleanness of hands, real purity of mind, real singleness of heart; let them learn a godly sorrow and penitence which will make them humble before God (4.6-10). And let them not forget that the more knowledge a man has, the greater his responsibility and the greater his guilt if he sins (3.1; 4.17).

(*f*) The greatest threat of all comes from the tongue (3.2-12). A little bit guides the horse, a little rudder steers the ship, a little spark sets the forest ablaze. Of all living things the tongue alone is beyond taming. The same tongue can bless God and curse men, which is as unnatural as it is for a fountain to produce both sweet and salt water. Let a man control the tongue, and he can control anything. Few men have been more aware of the peril of the uncontrolled tongue than James was.

It is in view of this that James preaches a religion of the most intensely practical character – and it is precisely that characterstic which will in due time lead us to the main problem of his Letter. True religion is to help the widow and the orphan and to keep oneself untarnished by the world (1.27). A man must be a doer of the word as well as a hearer of it, or his whole religion is an act of self-deception. The so-called wise man must demonstrate his alleged wisdom by showing it in his works. To bring one convert to Christ will cover a multitude of sins (1.22-25; 3.13; 5.19, 20).

But all these passages pale into comparative insignificance beside the almost belligerent passage on faith and works in 2.14-26.

Faith without works is dead, or, as the NEB renders it, faith that does not lead to action is a lifeless thing. What is the sense of expressing pious wishes for the feeding and the warming of a poor brother, and then doing nothing about it? Can anyone show his faith apart from his works? You say, I believe in God; you repeat the creed every day. The devils do the same and even tremble while they do so – but they are nonetheless devils for all that. Scripture itself shows the connection between faith and works. Abraham had faith in God and because of that faith he was prepared to sacrifice Isaac his son at the call of God; and it was precisely that *action* which proved the reality of his faith. It was by her *action* in protecting the Jewish scouts that Rahab was justified. The body without breath is dead; faith divorced from deeds is lifeless. Clearly, James is writing *con amore* with a passionate belief in what he is saying; and equally clearly James is writing the soundest commonsense. James instinctively sees law and religion walking hand in hand. Religion is the perfect law, the law of liberty, the law that makes men free (1.25). Religion is the royal law, the law that bids a man love his neighbor as himself (2.8).

The obvious question here is, Is James flatly, and perhaps even deliberately, contradicting Paul? Can a man's faith save him? demands James (2.14). Faith if it has no works is dead (2.17). It was Abraham's *action* in being willing to sacrifice Isaac that saved him (2.21-23). You see that a man is justified by works and not by faith alone (2.24). On the other hand we have Paul saying: 'We hold that a man is justified by faith apart from works of the Law' (Romans 3.28). 'A man is not justified by works of the Law but by faith in Jesus Christ ... for by the works of the Law no flesh shall be justified' (Galatians 2.16). The whole of Romans 4 is written precisely to prove that it was not by any work or works but by faith that Abraham was justified. Is Luther right? Is there here a flat contradiction which no amount of ingenuity can harmonize? There is no simple answer to this question, but there are certain things which we must note.

1. Jewish religion unquestionably believed that good works did matter and that a man could by his good deeds win the approval of God. 'All is according to the amount of work,' said Akiba (*Sayings of the Fathers* 3.19). 'It pleased God', said Rabbi Hananiah ben Akashya, 'to make Israel able to acquire merit; therefore he multiplied to them Law and commandment.' 'Let a man', says the Talmud, 'regard himself as if he were half-guilty and half-deserving, and then, if he fulfils one commandment, happy is he, for he has inclined the scale to merit; equally one sin will turn the scale the other way' (*Kid.*40 b). All the blessings are to those who are saved by their works; the righteous trust in them and are heard by God; Hezekiah trusted in his works, and had hope in his righteousness (II Baruch 51.7; 63.3). The righteous who have many good works laid up with God shall out of their deeds receive their reward (II Esdras 8.33). Every man shall find his reward before him according to his works (Sirach 16.14). These good works can even protect others. 'Your works', says Baruch, 'are to this city a firm pillar and your prayer a strong wall' (II Baruch 1.2). There is even a treasury of merit and the works of the patriarchs and the prophets will be available for their descendants.

But one question has to be asked – *What works?* There is no doubt as to the identity of the works in question.

> Alms to a father shall not be blotted out,
> And as a substitute for sin it shall be firmly planted.
> In the day of affliction it shall be remembered to thy credit;
> It shall obliterate thine iniquities as the heat the hoar frost.
>
> *(Sirach 3.14)*

Give alms of thy substance; turn not away from the face of any poor man, and the face of God shall not be turned away from thee. As thy substance is give alms of it, according to thine abundance; if thou have much, according to the abundance thereof, give alms; if thou have little bestow it, and be not afraid to give alms according to that little; for thou layest up a good treasure for thyself against the day of necessity; because alms delivereth from death, and suffereth not to come into darkness. Alms is a good offering in the sight of the Most High for all that give it.

(Tobit 4.7-11)

'Almsgiving', says the Talmud, 'is a powerful mediator between the Israelites and their Father in heaven; it brings the time of redemption nigh' (*Baba Bathra* 10 a).

All this is of the first importance, for it is quite clear that in the highest Jewish thought works are love in action, works are caring for our fellow-men. And the first and the simplest fact about James is that to him *works are never works of the Law*. He never mentions legalistic piety. His whole mind and heart and intention are fixed on the ethical works of mercy, justice, truth, loyalty, kindness and love. For James works are very nearly exactly what Paul meant by the fruit of the Spirit. James never even hinted that faith was expressed in, or a man justified by, what Paul called works of the Law.

2. It is equally true that James is thoroughly representative of NT thought. It is fruits fit for repentance John the Baptist demands (Matthew 3.8; Luke 3.8). All the world must see a Christian's good deeds and give the glory to God (Matthew 5.16). Men are known, like trees, by their fruits (Matthew 7.15-21).

No one in fact stressed this more strongly than Paul. Every one of his letters builds up to an ethical climax; his theology always ends in ethics. God will render to every man according to his deeds (Romans 2.6). Every man will give an account of himself to God (Romans 14.12). Every man will receive his own reward according to his labor (I Corinthians 3.8). We must all appear before the judgment seat of Christ that everyone may receive the things done in his body (II Corinthians 5.10). The *Didache* speaking of almsgiving says: 'If you have something to give, you can through your own hands give a ransom for your souls' (*Didache* 4).

The ethical stress is an absolutely essential part of NT teaching, and there are many passages in which Paul and James echo each other.

3. And yet the fact remains that there is a difference between the atmosphere of James and the atmosphere of Paul. Luther's reaction is proof enough of that. When all is said and done the emphasis of James is on works and the emphasis of Paul is on faith. What is the cause of this difference? Or, is there a real difference between them? To these questions there are two answers.

(*a*) It might well be not Paulinism but a perversion of Paulinism against which James's face was set. We have already seen, when we were studying the Gospel in Paul, that there is no easier doctrine to distort than the doctrine of grace; there were those who made grace simply an excuse for easy sinning. And it was always possible to misrepresent Paul into saying that all that mattered was faith and grace and that a man's actions were of no importance whatsoever.

(*b*) It is even more possible that what roused James's wrath was a misinterpretation of the meaning of the word faith. There are two kinds of faith. There is intellectual faith, in which a man accepts with his mind the mental proposition that something is true, but does not necessarily allow it to have any effect on his actions. And there is total faith, in which a man so commits himself to the confidence that something is true that it affects his whole life. To take a simple example, I believe that the square on the hypotenuse of a right-angled triangle is equal to the sum of the squares of the other two sides – but it makes no difference to me. But I believe that one and one make two and I will therefore steadily and strenuously refuse to pay two dollars fifty cents for two dollar articles.* The first kind of belief has no effect on my actions; the second kind of belief affects every one of my actions. This kind of thing can work in a slightly different way. I can believe that a thing is true and I can have a deep-down conviction that I ought to act on it, and yet I can refuse to act on it. Again to take an example, I may believe that the connection between smoking and lung-cancer is established; I may know well enough that I ought to stop smoking; and yet I may continue to smoke. Here again belief has failed to affect action.

Now it may well be that James is preaching against that kind of faith which is academic acceptance of a proposition or even conviction that something is true, *without accompanying action*. This is certainly not Pauline faith, for, as we have seen, Pauline faith is committal to a person and his promises and demands. But nonetheless the other kind of faith always has been, and is still, tragically common, and James may well be condemning, not Paul, but those who either in ignorance misunderstood, or by design misinterpreted, the Pauline doctrines of grace and faith.

(c) It is maybe even more likely that Paul and James are speaking about different stages of the Christian faith. When Paul said that no man can ever get into a right relationship with God through works he is certainly thinking of the *initial step* of the Christian life. He is thinking of that moment when a man abandons the vain delusion that he can do something to save himself, and casts himself unreservedly on the mercy and the love of God. In that moment a man well knows that works are irrelevant and that all that matters is the love of God. Now

---

* converted for year 2000 currencies

clearly James is thinking of a much later stage in the Christian life; he is thinking of the man who has taken that decision, who has made that committal, and who has set out upon the Christian way. In other words he is thinking in terms of sanctification far more than in terms of justification. We have already drawn the distinction, and here we see the difference in action. It remains for ever true that a man is not saved *by* works, but he is saved *for* works. By no means can a man's good deeds save him; but equally by no means can a man be called a Christian if his so-called committal to Christ has had no ethical effect upon his life, for the simple reason that, if there is no ethical effect on his life, his committal is not true committal. With this Paul would whole-heartedly have agreed, for this is the very thing that he kept saying over and over again.

The real fact is that there is no contradiction between Paul and James other than a purely verbal one, and that contradiction only appears if the whole background of thought is neglected. Paul and James are not antithetic and contradictory; they are complementary and mutually completing. They are not to be set over against each other, as if it was a case of 'either, or'; they are to be taken together, because it is a case of 'both, and'. In the beginning works cannot save a man; in the end a man is saved for works. The initial movement is a casting oneself on God; the steady progress is an ethical advancement, and in a pagan society James was right, for the Gospel which wins men is the Gospel of practical action which demonstrates that men are redeemed.

7
First Peter

The Gospel of Obligation

The pervading characteristic of the First Letter of Peter is its tremendous sense of the obligation which the work of Christ has laid upon the Christian. Peter hardly ever mentions a gift which the Christian has received without insisting on the responsibility and the obligation which go with it. The Good News has come to Christians, news of things into which the angels long to look, therefore they must gird up their minds and be sober in hope and in obedience (1.10-14). He who has called them is holy, therefore they must be holy too (1.15, 16). They have been given the great privilege of calling God Father, therefore they must walk in godly fear (1.17). At great cost they have been ransomed from their futile ways, therefore they must purify their souls by their obedience (1.18-22). The word of God, the Good News, has been preached to them, therefore they must put away all malice and all guile and all unchristian things (1.25-2.1). At the moment they may be babes, but they must grow up into salvation because they have experienced the kindness of God (2.2). They are a chosen race, a royal priesthood, a holy nation, therefore they must live with the discipline of strangers and pilgrims (2.9-11). Since Jesus Christ lived in uncomplaining meekness, whatever men might do to him, therefore the Christian servant must do the same (2.18-25). Christ died for the righteous and the unrighteous, therefore the Christian must be prepared to suffer for the right (3.17, 18).

Because Jesus Christ suffered when he was on this earth in a mortal body, therefore the Christian must arm himself with the same intention (4.1, 2). The Christian must keep sane and sober for his prayers because the end of the world is at hand (4.7). As E. G. Selwyn puts it, the Christian believer is a man who has 'the Lord's example behind him, and the hope of glory in front of him', and by these two things the tone and character of his life is dominated and dictated. All through the letter there runs this constant sense of the obligation and the responsibility which the mercy and the grace and the love of God in Jesus Christ have laid upon the Christian.

As Peter sees it, this obligation of the Christian extends in another direction. The Christian is deeply involved in the world; no NT book is less other-worldly than First Peter. As E. G. Selwyn puts it, it was the conviction of Peter that the Christian by his patience, his suffering and his activity in life 'should mould society into closer conformity with the will of God'. Selwyn quotes a saying of Toynbee which well expresses Peter's point of view: 'The antithesis between trying to save one's own soul by seeking and following God, and trying to do one's duty to one's neighbor, is false. The two activities are indissoluble.'

Because of this no one in the NT is more aware than Peter of the fact that a Christian life is far and away the best apologetic for, and commendation of, Christianity. In a time of hostility and persecution Christianity's only defence is Christianity. To put it very crudely, Peter is vividly aware of the propaganda value of the Christian life. If the heathen malign the Christians, the Christian's answer must be his good deeds (2.12). It is by doing right that the Christian must put to silence the ignorance of foolish men (2.15). A wife by the sheer radiant loveliness of her life must, without a word ever being spoken, be the means of her heathen husband's conversion (3.1, 2). The conscience of the Christian must be so clear and his behavior must be so Christlike that he will put to shame those who revile Christ and Christianity (3.16). No Christian must ever suffer as a murderer, a thief, a criminal, a mischief-maker (4.15). The only defence the Christian has, and the supreme missionary weapon a Christian possesses, must be the example and the demonstration of a Christian life.

Because of this it has been said that Peter has an *exemplarist* Christology. An exemplarist Christology is a view of Jesus Christ, which sees in him a great example whose moral power has a changing effect on men; it sees in Jesus Christ, not a sacrifice and not a reconciliation, but an example and a pattern, so magnetic and so powerful that it transforms men into its own image. Is it then true that Peter sees in Jesus no more than a dynamic example?

In the first place, we must return to something which we mentioned at the beginning of this book. Men of different temperaments will necessarily have a difference in the character of their religion. Charles Bigg in his commentary on I Peter draws a very useful distinction between the two main temperaments, the temperament of the *Mystic* and the temperament of the *Disciplinarian*:

A Disciplinarian is one who hears God speaking to him; a Mystic is one who feels the presence of God within. The former says, 'Christ is my Savior, Shepherd, Friend, my Judge, my Rewarder'; the latter says, 'Not I live, but Christ liveth in me'. The former sedulously distinguishes the human personality from the divine; the latter desires to sink his own personality in the divine. Hence the leading Disciplinarian ideas are Grace considered as a gift, Law, Learning, Continuity, Godly Fear – in all these human responsibility is steadily kept in view. But the leading Mystic ideas are Grace as an indwelling power, Freedom, the Inner Light,

Discontinuity (Law and Gospel, Flesh and Spirit, World and God).

This differentiation is essentially true, and most of us will easily recognize ourselves as belonging to one or other of these categories. To put the matter at its widest, Paul is the typical Mystic and Peter is the typical Disciplinarian. Therefore, Peter will always stress the responsibility and the ethical obligation of Christianity, and will always see in Jesus Christ an example, however much more he sees, while Paul will always think in terms of inner communion and unity with Jesus Christ.

This can be well seen in Peter's way of speaking of *faith* and of *salvation*. The Christian is guarded through faith for a salvation ready to be revealed at the last time. (1.5). A true and genuine faith is like metal tried, tested and purified in the fire (1.7). As the outcome of his faith the Christian receives the salvation of his soul (1.9). It is the power of God demonstrated in the resurrection of Jesus Christ 'which gives us faith and hope in him (1.21). The Christian must resist the devil, firm in his faith (5.9). Peter's readers are babes in the faith, but they must grow up into salvation (2.2). From this it emerges that for Peter faith is a combination of unshakable loyalty and equally unshakable hope. It is not for Peter, as it is for Paul, a kind of inner union with Jesus Christ; it is rather deathless loyalty responding to deathless love in immortal hope. Salvation for Peter is something which is at the end of the road, rather than it is for Paul a present experience. Someone has put it like this. For Paul religion is 'an experience which ends in an experiment' and for Peter 'religion is an experiment which ends in an experience'. Peter had no Damascus road. He began by following Jesus and in that following had a progressive experience of the wonder of Jesus Christ. Paul would have said: 'I came in a flash to know Jesus Christ, and then I set out on the

Christian way.' Peter would have said: 'I set out on the Christian way, and the longer I walk it the more I know and love my Lord.' But let us return to our question. If this to say that for Peter Jesus is mainly a magnetic example? We can answer that question by looking at the pictures in which Peter thinks of Jesus.

1. To Peter Jesus is *the perfect example*. He left us an example that we should follow in his steps (2.21). The word is *hupogrammos*, and it means the line of copperplate handwriting at the top of the page of a writing exercise-book, which the scholar must copy as best he can. Jesus is the pattern for life which the Christian must ever try to reproduce.

2. To Peter Jesus is *Lord*. In your hearts, he says, reverence Christ as Lord (3.15). The word is *kurios*. It means the absolute master and owner of any person or thing; it is the word used for the Roman Emperor; it is the word which in the Greek OT is used to translate the name of God. To Peter Jesus is the undisputed Lord and Master of his life, to whom is owed an absolute loyalty and an absolute obedience and a humble worship.

3. To Peter Jesus is *the Stone*. Peter works this out fully in 2.6-8. He uses three OT quotations. He quotes Isaiah 28.16 where it is God's expressed intention to lay a tested cornerstone, a sure foundation. He quotes Psalm 118.22 which speaks of the stone which was rejected but which has become the head of the corner. He quotes Isaiah 8.14, 15 which speaks of the stone over which men will stumble and fall. So then to Peter Jesus is the only sure foundation of life; he is the one whom men rejected but who is to become head over all; he is the one over whom the unbeliever will stumble to ruin but on whom the believer will build his life.

4. To Peter Jesus is *the Judge*. Men will give account to him who is ready to judge the living and the dead (4.5). Jesus is not

only the pattern in this life; he is also the judge in the life to come.

5. To Peter Jesus is *the Shepherd*. Pasture in Palestine was scanty and hard to find. Such pasture as there was was surrounded with deserts and cliffs in which the straying sheep might perish of hunger and thirst or over which it might plunge to disaster. The shepherd had to be for ever on the watch day and night, and had to be at any time ready to risk his life to seek and to find the sheep which had strayed away. Jesus is the sentinel of his people's safety and the rescuer of their lost souls at the cost of his own life.

6. So far it would be possible to class Peter as an exemplarist, and so far it is not necessary to see in Jesus anything other than a great example. But now we come on two pictures which lift the whole matter on to another plane.

To Peter Jesus was *the Passover Lamb*. Christians have been redeemed, not by any human currency of silver and gold, but by the precious blood of Christ, like that of a lamb without blemish and without spot (1.18, 19; cp. Exodus 12.5). The reference to the lamb without blemish and without spot can hardly be anything other than a reference to the Passover lamb (Exodus 12.1-27). And it was the blood of that lamb smeared upon the lintel and the doorposts of their houses which kept the people of Israel safe when the angel of death strode in destruction through the land of Egypt. So then it is the blood of Jesus Christ, the sacrifice of his life, which saves his people from their sins, and from the judgment of God.

7. To Peter Jesus was *the scapegoat*. It is most probable that this is the picture in the mind of Peter, when he speaks of Jesus bearing our sins in his own body to the tree, or on the tree (2.24). The scapegoat (or, as the modern translations more correctly have it, the goat for Azazel) was part of the ritual of the Day of Atonement (Leviticus 16.6-10, 20-22). At a certain

stage in the ritual the High Priest confessed all the iniquities and transgressions of the people with his hands resting on the head of the goat. The sins of the people were then, as it were, transferred to the goat. The goat was then sent away and bore 'all their iniquities upon him to a solitary land'. In some way the sins of the people were transferred to the animal and thus borne away. Even so Jesus bore upon himself the sins of mankind.

8. To Peter Jesus was the *Suffering Servant* of Isaiah 53. Peter says of Jesus:

> He commited no sin; no guile was found on his lips. When he was reviled, he did not revile in return; when he suffered, he did not threaten; but he trusted to him who judges justly. He himself bore our sins in his body on the tree, that we might die to sin and live to righteousness. By his wounds you have been healed. For you were like straying sheep, but have now returned to the Shepherd and Guardian of your souls (2.22-25).

Here Jesus is distinctly seen in terms of the Suffering Servant, and the Suffering Servant, however mysterious a figure he may be, was one whose vicarious sufferings were for the sake of the healing of his people.

9. To Peter Jesus is *the Guardian of our souls* (2.25). The word is *episkopos*, and the AV, now misleadingly, translates the word *bishop*. *Episkopos* literally means *one who watches over*. It can be used quite simply in the sense of a taskmaster (Isaiah 60.17). But it can also be used in the sense of a *guardian*. In Rhodes there were five *episkopoi*, whose task it was to be the guardians of the rights and privileges of the whole community. God, says Philo, is the *episkopos* of the universe. Heaven is the *episkopos* of all men, and the stars are a thousand eyes which look down and keep watch. So then to Peter Jesus is the Guardian and the Protector of the souls of men.

It can easily be seen that Peter has a far more than

exemplarist view of the work of Jesus Christ. True, he sees Jesus as example, but he sees him also as the Savior who died to deliver men from sin, and as the risen Lord who lives to guard, to shepherd and to guide.

Out of all the riches of I Peter we have space to choose only one other line of thought. I Peter was clearly written in a time of suffering and of trial (1.6; 3.14; 4.12-14). It was probably written at a time when the savagery of persecution was just beginning to break upon the Christian Church. It is therefore of very special interest to see what it has to say about the Christian attitude to suffering.

1. Suffering, as Peter sees it, is not something which should come to the Christian as a surprise; it is an integral and inevitable part of the Christian situation, which a man should expect and for which he should be prepared (4.12).

2. The Christian must never suffer as a criminal or a wrong-doer (4.15). One of the great tests of any man is his reaction to undeserved and unjust suffering (2.20; 3.17). It is as a Christian that the Christian will suffer, for in the days of Peter the Christian's only crime was Christ (4.14, 16).

3. To suffer ought to give a man a sense of unity with those who throughout the world are undergoing the same experiences (5.9). To suffer for the right is to undergo an experience as old as time and as wide as the world.

4. Suffering provides one of the basic tests of life. It is not simply an experience; it is an ordeal (4.12); and a faith which has really stood the test is like precious metal tried and purified in the fire (1.6, 7). Suffering is neither purposeless nor profitless; it is designed to produce a life and character that a trouble-free existence could never create.

5. To suffer is to experience unity with the experience of Jesus Christ. In his suffering he left us an example that we should follow in his steps (2.21). To suffer for doing right is

exactly to repeat the experience of Jesus himself (3.17, 18); and to share the sufferings of Jesus is something which should make a Christian rejoice (4.13). A common experience of suffering forges an intimate bond between sufferers, and it is that way between the Christian and Christ.

6. The acceptance of suffering for the right and for Christ certainly brings blessedness to follow (3.14). If we share the sufferings of Christ, we shall assuredly share the glory of Christ (4.13; 5.10). God will be in no man's debt; there is in life a law of ultimate compensation. Without the cross there can be no crown; but with the cross the crown is certain.

7. Therefore, the ultimate duty is to do right and to trust in God (4.19). To trust in God and do the right would be not far from being a summary of Peter's message.

And this all the more so because the eyes of the Christian are ever upon the beyond. It is true that the Christian is deeply involved in the world; but nonetheless there is a real sense in which he is in the world as an exile (1.17). He is an alien and an exile, a stranger and a pilgrim (2.11). The world matters, and it matters for the very reason that it points beyond itself. The Christian is at once the gladiator of time and the pilgrim of eternity. As the apocryphal saying of Jesus has it: 'The world is a bridge. The wise man will pass over it, but he will not build his house upon it.'

It remains to look at one doctrine which has its special source and origin in I Peter. In the Apostles' Creed it is said of Jesus 'He descended into hell' and the doctrine in question is known as the Descent into Hell. There are two passages in First Peter which are the basis of that doctrine:

Christ also died for sins once for all, the righteous for the unrighteous, that he might bring us to God, being put to death in the flesh, but made alive in the spirit; *in which he went and*

preached to the spirits in prison, who formerly did not obey, when
God's patience waited in the days of Noah (3.18-20).

This is why the Gospel was preached even to the dead (4.6).

It is on the basis of these and certain other NT passages that the
doctrine of the Descent into Hell is founded.

We must begin by noting that the expression the Descent into
Hell begins with the wrong idea. Correctly, we ought to speak
of the Descent into Hades, for whatever this line of thought
actually came to mean, it began by meaning, not that Jesus
descended into the place of punishment, but that Jesus
descended into the place where according to Jewish thought *all*
the dead go. The Jews had no firm belief in the after-life. They
believed that all the dead went to the same place where they
lived a gray, shadowy, strengthless existence, like ghosts and
wraiths, separated from man and God alike (Psalm 6.5; 39.13;
88.10-12; 115.17; Ecclesiastes 9.4, 5, 10). True, there were
brief glimpses of a higher belief and of a communion with God
which not even death could sever (Psalm 16.8-11; 17.15; 49.10-
15; 73.23, 24; Job 14.7-14; 19.25-27; Isaiah 26.19; Daniel
12.2, 3), but the orthodox Jewish belief was that Hades or the
Pit was the twilight land to which all the dead went. It is to that
place of the dead that the doctrine originally held that Jesus
went between his crucifixion and his resurrection. The other
passages in which some reference to this doctrine may be found
are Acts 2.27; Romans 10.6, 7; Ephesians 4.8-10; John 5.25;
Philippians 2.9-11; Revelation 5.13.

There are certain interpretations of I Peter 3.18-20 which
eliminate the doctrine altogether.

1. It has been suggested that what the passage means is that
Christ through the Spirit preached to the men of Noah's time in
Noah's time when they were still alive and sinning upon this

earth. It has already been said that the Spirit of Christ spoke through the prophets (1.10-12), and it is suggested that in and through the Spirit Christ preached to the men of Noah's time and unsuccessfully pled with them to repent. 3.18-20 could mean this, but certainly 4.6 could not.

2. It has been suggested that *the spirits in prison* are the rebellious angels mentioned in II Peter 2.4, and are not men at all, and that to them Christ preached final doom and condemnation.

3. It has been suggested that the word *Enoch* has dropped out. This suggestion, made by Rendel Harris, is accepted by Moffatt who renders:

> In the flesh he was put to death, but he came to life in the Spirit. It was in the Spirit that Enoch also went and preached to the imprisoned spirits who disobeyed at the time when God's patience held out during the construction of the ark in the days of Noah.[1]

It is in fact the case that Enoch plays a very important part in the intertestamental literature, and that in that literature he is actually depicted as announcing their doom to the rebellious

---

1 The explanation offered for the alleged omission of the word Enoch is as follows. We transliterate the Greek and under each Greek word put its English translation:

thanatōtheis		*sarki*		*zōopoiētheis*	
Having been put to death		in the flesh		having been raised to life	
pneumati	*en hō*	*kai*	*tois*	*en phulakē*	*pneumasin*
in the spirit	in which	also	to the	in prison	spirits
poreutheis		*ekēruxen*			
having gone		he preached.			

When two very similar looking or sounding words came together it was by no means uncommon for the scribes who copied the manuscripts accidentally to omit one of them. So it is suggested that the original text ran *en hō kai Enōch*, and that *en hō kai* sounds so like *Enōch*, that the word *Enōch* was omitted in copying.

angels. But there is not in fact the slightest evidence that Enoch ever stood in the text and this suggestion must be discarded.

Assuming then that the passage does mean that Jesus went to the place of the dead, what interpretations of it have been suggested?

1. Calvin took it in the sense that Jesus did descend to Hell, the place of punishment, and that in Hell he actually bore the pains of Hell which all men should have borne. 'He bore that death which is inflicted by God on sinners.' That interpretation cannot be accepted because the place to which Jesus descended was Hades and not Hell.

2. In the early Church the commonest of all interpretations was that Jesus descended to the place of the dead and preached the Gospel to the patriarchs, the saints, the prophets and the martyrs of the OT, and then lead them out of Hades into heaven. He went, as Tertullian put it (*On the Soul* 55), that he might make the patriarchs and prophets partakers of himself.

3. This was developed by Clement of Alexandria (*The Miscellanies* 2.2; 6.6) who extended the preaching of Jesus in the place of the dead to those Gentiles who had lived in righteousness according to the law and philosophy. Clement had always seen in pagan philosophy, and especially in Greek philosophy, a very real preparation for Christ, and in the Descent he saw the philosophers receive their opportunity to hear the Gospel. This is one of the most beautiful, attractive and adventurous ideas to which early Christian thought ever attained.

4. In its most developed form the Descent into Hades became the Harrowing of Hell in which death is finally defeated, Hell harrowed, and all the saints set free.

5. Attractive and dramatic as many of these ideas are, it is very unlikely that they are what the doctrine originally meant. The phrase *he descended into hell* is not in the Nicene Creed,

nor is it in the confession of the Eastern Orthodox Church. Rufinus, one of the very early fifth century commentators on the creed, noted that this phrase was in neither the Roman nor the Eastern creed, and he held that it was simply another way of saying that Jesus was really and truly dead, that he did in every way experience death. As Tertullian put it, 'By remaining in Hades he fully complied with the form and condition of a dead man' (*On the Soul*, 55). There were those in the early Church who so stressed the divinity of Christ and so neglected the manhood of Christ that they held that he only seemed to suffer and die. It was against them that this article was inserted into the creed, with the intention of affirming the faith of the Church that Jesus Christ really and truly experienced death for the sake of the men whom he came to save.

So Peter with an extraordinary completeness presents us with the Christ who pre-existed in history and before history began (1.10, 11, 20), the Christ who came to this earth and who suffered and died for men on the cross (1.16-22; 2.24), the Christ who descended into Hades and so tasted the full bitterness of death (3.19), the Christ who rose from death (1.3, 21; 3.21), the Christ who ascended into glory (1.11; 3.22), and the Christ who will come again (1.7, 13; 4.7; 5.1, 4).

8
The Letter of John

The Gospel of Right Belief and True Love

Although I John is called a letter it neither begins nor ends as such. And yet no work was ever more clearly addressed to a definite community by an author who knew intimately and loved passionately those to whom he wrote. I John is in fact rather a homily than a letter, and it was written by one in whose heart the pastoral instinct was dominant above all other things. 'The writer', says A. E. Brooke, 'may or may not have been a theologian. Undoubtedly he *was* the pastor of his flock. His chief interest is the care of souls.' It is, says Westcott, 'instinct from first to last with personal feeling. The writer is not dealing with abstractions but with life and living men.'

He was writing at a time when the enemy was within the gates and when the Church was threatened from within. The danger did not come from persecution or from any threat from outside the Church. It came from mistaken teachers who had been within the Church, although now they have seceded from the Church (2.19). John has much to say about the world. The Christian is not to love the world or the things in the world; if he does the Father is not in him (2.15-17). The world does not recognize the Christian because it did not recognize Christ and does not know God (3.1). It is only to be expected that the world should hate the Church (3.13). The false teachers are of the world and naturally the world listens to them, but we are of God (4.4, 5). The danger is not the danger of persecution; it is the danger of assimilation to the world. The world has become too attractive; philosophy and speculation and adjustment of Christian belief to contemporary thought have become too fascinating; the clean-cut distinction between the Christian and the world has become irksome and burdensome. The curious thing about I John is that it comes from an age when the first instinct of the pastor is no longer to go out and to win the world, but rather to withdraw from the world, lest the infection of the world should so taint the Church that Christianity should become simply another syncretistic faith and not the unique and only word of God. For that reason I John has three great characteristics.

1. It is consistently *polemical*. Robert Law says: 'There is no NT writing which is more vigorously polemical in its whole tone and aim. The truth, which in the same writer's Gospel, shines as the dayspring from on high, becomes here a searchlight, flashed into a background of darkness.' John is waging a holy war on a falsehood which could wreck the faith.

2. It is none the less written equally for *edification*. It is never simply invective. If it wishes to destroy the enemies of the faith, it equally wishes to build up the children of the faith. A. E. Brooke writes: 'Although John never loses sight of his opponents, the aim is not primarily polemical; it is edification . . . The aim is not so much the defeat of the opponents as the building up of a correct attitude in the children to Christian faith and life.' Poison has to be eradicated but true food has to be supplied.

3. The ever-recurring note of the letter is *recall to that which is already known*. The constant plea of John to his people is: 'Be what you really are.' They know him who is from the beginning (2.13, 14). They have been anointed by the Holy One and they already know (2.20). He writes, not because they do not know the truth, but because they already know it (2.21). They do not really need anyone to teach them (2.27). They know that Jesus

Christ has appeared to take away sins (3.5). They know and believe the love that God has for them (4.16). They know that they are of God and that God has given them understanding (5.19, 20). The whole point of the letter is not to instruct the ignorant, but to recall people to that which they already know, and to urge them to be what they in fact are.

In view of all this we must begin our study of John's letter by seeing the nature of the teaching which constituted so grave a threat to the Christian faith and Church. That teaching belonged to that general type of thought that is called Gnosticism. What then were the characteristic Gnostic beliefs?

1. Epiphanius says that Basilides, one of the greatest of the Gnostic thinkers, began with the question: 'Whence comes evil?' (*pothen to kakon*). Gnosticism found its explanation of evil in a thorough-going dualism. It held that spirit, which is God, and matter are both eternal; that spirit is altogether good; that matter has from the beginning a flaw in it; and that out of that flawed matter the world has been made. As Robert Law puts it: 'Gnosticism traces into the eternal the schism of which we are conscious in the world of experience, and posits two independent and antagonistic principles of existence from which, severally, come all the good and all the evil that exist.'

2. Since matter is essentially evil the God who is pure spirit cannot touch it. This god therefore puts out a series of aeons or emanations, each a little more removed and distant from himself. As the emanations grow more distant from the true God they grow more ignorant of the true God. As they grow still more distant, they become not only ignorant but hostile to the true God. At the end of the series there comes a power distant from, ignorant of, hostile to, the true God and that power is the creator of the world. As Robert Law put it: 'Gnostic evolution is from divinity downwards.' Thus the world is created out of flawed material and by a power who is the

ignorant enemy of the true God. Hence come the sin and suffering of the world and all its imperfections.

3. This doctrine has certain ethical results.

(a) It completely does away with any Christian doctrine of sin, for sin is no longer the result of a moral choice made in rebellion against God by the mind and the heart of man; sin is simply a physical principle in matter and in all that is composed of matter. Any physical creature or thing is bound to sin because of its physical composition. It is quite impossible to change or renew its nature; the only thing which can stop sin is the total destruction of all physical and material things, until only spirit, which is good, is left.

(b) In practice this issues in one of two attitudes to life.

First, it may issue in a rigid asceticism. If the body and all physical things are essentially evil, then the body must be subdued and its every need and desire must be refused.

Second, it may issue in a kind of licence to sin on either of two grounds. If the body is evil, then it does not matter anyway what we do with it for nothing can make it good. Therefore, let the body have its way. If in nature there is this split, then let spirit and body each go its own way. Let each act according to its own nature. Let spirit reach out to goodness, and let the body sin to its heart's content, then each will be fulfilling its own nature. And, in any event, a really spiritual man will not be in the least affected by what his body does. In fact the more spiritual a man is, the less it makes any difference if his body sins.

4. The way of escape is knowledge. The spirit of man is imprisoned in the evil flesh of the body, and only a special kind of knowledge can enable the spirit to escape from the body. The long way to God has to be climbed, past all the aeons and the emanations; there are necessary secret instructions, secret passwords, secret knowledge. At the heart of Gnosticism there is this

necessity for special and esoteric knowledge. The Gnostics divided men into two classes, the *pneumatikoi*, the spiritual ones, for whom such knowledge is a possibility and to whom such knowledge is open, and the *psuchikoi*, those who, as it were, have no more than an animal soul, and for whom such knowledge is impossible and to whom such knowledge is a closed book. Gnosticism inevitably and deliberately issued in a situation in which there were an intellectual aristocracy and an ignorant and unteachable majority.

The consequence is quite clear; Gnosticism was the death of fellowship. In its arid intellectualism it killed love. Robert Law says of it: 'The system was loveless to the core.' Ignatius (*The Letter to Smyrna* 6.2) says of the Gnostics of his day: 'They give no heed to love, caring not for the widow, the orphan, the afflicted, neither for those who are in bonds, neither for the hungry nor the thirsty.' There can be no fellowship where there is an intellectual *élite*, and a great majority of simple folk who are despised, and where a man's aim is to know rather than to love.

5. It is quite clear that this kind of belief was bound to have the most serious consequences for Christology. No Gnostic could possibly believe in a real incarnation; he could not believe that the Son of the true God could ever take upon himself a body which is essentially evil. So the Gnostics were Docetists, which literally means *Seemists*. Sometimes they held that Jesus only seemed to have a body, and that in fact he was no more than a spiritual phantom. In the Acts of John, for instance, it is said that when Jesus walked he left no footprints on the ground. No Gnostic could possibly have said that the Word became flesh. Sometimes they held that, since the true God can never suffer, the spiritual Christ descended upon the man Jesus in the form of a dove at his baptism; Jesus then perfected his virtues and announced the Father; but before his sufferings and death

the Christ withdrew again from the man Jesus, and it was only the man Jesus who suffered and died and rose again. No Gnostic could believe in a flesh and blood Christ, and no Gnostic could believe in a divine being who knew suffering and death.

Let us now go to the Letter itself and let us see if we can discover from it what the erroneous views of the false teachers were.

1. Their teaching about Jesus was false and dangerous.

(*a*) They denied that Jesus was the Christ (2.22), and, conversely, every one who believes that Jesus is the Christ is a child of God (5.1). This is not to be taken as a denial that Jesus was the Messiah. It means that, as we have seen that many Gnostics did say, that the heavenly Christ only came into the man Jesus for a limited time, that the Christ came upon the man Jesus at the baptism and left him before the suffering and death of the Cross. In the Gospel of Peter the cry on the Cross: 'My God, my God, why have you forsaken me?' becomes: 'My Power, my Power, why have you forsaken me?' and is taken to be the lament of the man Jesus that the heavenly Christ has left him.

It is this same belief which explains the strange saying in 5.6: 'This is he who came by water and blood, Jesus Christ, not with water only, but with the water and the blood.' The point is that the heretics were quite prepared to say that the Christ came into Jesus at the Baptism, that is, with water; but they were not prepared to say that the Christ was in Jesus at his death on the Cross, that is, with the blood. In a word, the heretics so sought to protect the glory of God that they found it impossible to associate God and suffering, and they thereby despoiled God of his supreme glory, which is his suffering love.

(*b*) The heretics denied the fulness of the incarnation; they refused to believe that Jesus came in the flesh (4.2, 3). It was the incarnation that any Gnostic was bound to deny. They could not believe that God could take manhood upon him, and so they presented men with a Jesus who was no more than a phantom in human shape. They thereby destroyed the work of Christ for, as Irenaeus said, 'He became what we are to make us what he is.' Docetism in a kind of mistaken reverence took the meaning out of the life of Jesus Christ.

2. Their ethical teaching was wrong and dangerous. They claimed to have fellowship with God and yet they walked in darkness (1.5). That is to say, they claimed to be walking with God and yet went on sinning. They in fact denied that they sinned at all (1.8-10). They would have said that a truly spiritual man may allow his body to do as it likes, for his body thereby simply fulfils its nature, and that cannot be called sin. John insists that no one who abides in God sins, that the righteous man is he who does righteousness. No one born of God commits sin, for sin is of the Devil (3.6-10). To love God is to keep God's commandments (5.3). He who is born of God does not sin (5.18). This is directed against the Gnostics who claimed that they were in the most intimate possible fellowship with God, fellowship not even possible for the ordinary man, and who yet wallowed in sin, either on the principle that the body is evil and therefore it does not matter what is done with it or in it, or on the principle that in sin the body does no more than fulfil its own nature, and that in either case the spirit is left quite untouched. To the Gnostics an unethical religion was perfectly natural; to John it was a blasphemous contradiction in terms.

3. Their personal relationships were quite unchristian, for the whole principle of their lives was, not love, but contempt and hatred for their fellow-men. The original message of Christianity is that we should love one another (3.11). Belief in Christ and love of man must go hand in hand (3.23). Anyone who does not love is spiritually dead, and he who hates his

brother is in effect a murderer (3.14, 15). The man who hates his brother, whatever claims he may make, is still in the darkness (2.9-11). The man who claims to love God and who at the same time hates his brother is a liar (4.20). To the Gnostics contempt for and hatred of the common man were part and parcel of religion; to John they were the complete negation of Christianity.

Let us now go on to see what John regards as true religion. Robert Law's valuable exposition of I John is entitled *The Tests of Life*, and one of the features of John's Letter is the fact that it does provide a series of tests in a series of sayings all beginning with some such phrase as, 'By this we know.' Let us look at these tests, of which there are five.

1. There is *the ethical test*. 'By this we may be sure that we know him, if we keep his commandments . . . By this we may be sure that we are in him: he who says he abides in him ought to walk in the same way in which he walked' (2.3-6). 'If you know that he is righteous, you may be sure that everyone who does right is born of him' (2.29). 'By this it may be seen who are the children of God, and who are the children of the devil; whoever does not do right is not of God' (3.10). 'By this we know that we love the children of God, when we love God and obey his commandments' (5.2). The unique characteristic of John is what can only be called an *ethical mysticism*. Abiding in God and obeying God are one and the same thing. After all, the only real test of love is obedience. And John never forgot that Jesus Christ came 'to make bad men good.'

2. There is *the theological test*. 'By this you know the spirit of God. Every spirit that confesses that Jesus Christ is come in the flesh is of God, and every spirit that does not confess Jesus is not of God. This is the spirit of antichrist' (4.2, 3). 'Whoever confesses that Jesus is the Son of God, God abides in him and he in God' (4.15). Only when the center of the circle is right can the

circumference be right. At the center of man's life there must be a true appreciation of Jesus Christ; and it is significant that for John the supreme danger lies in losing sight of the manhood of Jesus. Of all the NT writers he clings most tenaciously to the historical Jesus, that which 'we have heard, we have seen with our eyes, which we have looked upon and touched with our hands' (1.1, 2). John quite certainly would have regarded with horror any line of thought which evaporated the historical, flesh and blood man Jesus out of Christianity.

3. There is *the spiritual test*. 'By this we know that he abides in us, by the Spirit who he has given us' (3.24). 'By this we know that we abide in him, and he in us, because he has given us of his own Spirit' (4.13). To get the full greatness of this we would have to turn back to the Fourth Gospel and see again the greatness of the promise of the Spirit in the fourteenth and the sixteenth chapters. For John the life of the Christian is characterized by a power that is more than human. It should be possible for the man of the world to look at the man of Christ and to be compelled to say: 'Here is life such as I have never known and life which I want to know.'

4. There is the test of *receptiveness*. 'Whoever knows God listens to us, and he who is not of God does not listen to us. By this we know the spirit of truth and the spirit of error' (4.6). The word of God, when it is preached to men, is not only a promise and an offer, it is also a judgment. A man reveals himself in his response to the Gospel of God in Jesus Christ.

5. Above and beyond all else, there is *the test of love*. 'By this it may be seen who are the children of God, and who are the children of the devil; whoever does not do right is not of God; nor he who does not love his brother' (3.9). 'We know that we have passed out of death into life because we love the brethren' (3.14). Unquestionably the key-note of John's letter is love, and to end our study of it we must look at this love.

(*a*) Love is the original message of the Christian faith (3.11). It is the very foundation stone of the Christian life.

(*b*) To love is to abide in the light (2.10); and, conversely, to fail to love is to be alienated from God, to be in spiritual death, and to make one's profession a lie (3.10; 3.14; 4.20).

(*c*) There is a false love, the love of the world (2.15), but such a love can only separate a man from God.

(*d*) This love must be practically shown. To see a brother in need and not to help him out of our own fulness makes any profession of love a lie (3.17, 18). Fine words and emotions can never replace fine deeds.

(*e*) The only test of true love is obedience (5.2, 3). To love God is to keep his commandments, and his great commandment is to love one another.

(*f*) Belief and love go hand in hand. We must believe in Jesus Christ and love one another (3.23). He who loves God must love his brother also (4.21). The only way in which any man can prove that he loves God is by loving his fellow-men.

(*g*) True love is seen in God and in God's sacrifice for us in his Son (3.16; 4.9). It is because God is love that we must love, and in loving we become kin to God (4.7, 8, 16, 19). It is God's love for us that lays on us the compulsion to love one another (4.19). He who is loved is under obligation to love. And John has a very great thought. No man has ever seen God; but in love God can be seen; human love, imperfect as it always must be, is a glimpse into the heart of God (4.12).

The Letter of John is as contemporary today as on the day on which it was first written. It forbids at one and the same time a selfish mysticism and an arid intellectualism. It sees in Christianity a union between right belief and true love, a union in which there is a meeting of the seeking mind and the loving heart in Christ.

9

II Peter and Jude

The Gospel of the Good Life

There are very few ordinary Christian people who are familiar with the Second Letter of Peter and the Letter of Jude. They are both books which for long stood rather on the fringe of the NT than as an integral and undoubted part of it. Eusebius always speaks of them with a doubt. When he was writing of the writings of Peter, Eusebius said that I Peter is everywhere unquestioningly received, but, 'We have learned that his extant Second Letter does not belong to the canon; yet it has appeared profitable to many, and it has been used with the other Scriptures'. He speaks of the doubt concerning the Letter of James, and then he goes on to say: 'At least not many of the ancients have mentioned it, as is the case likewise with the Letter that bears the name of Jude . . . We nevertheless know that these also with the rest have been read publicly in very many Churches.' In his classification of the NT books he writes: 'Among the disputed writings, which are nevertheless recognized by many, are extant the so-called Letter of James, and that of Jude, also the Second Letter of Peter.' He quotes the verdict of Origen: 'Peter has left one acknowledged letter; perhaps also a second, but this is doubtful' (*The Ecclesiastical History* 3.3.1; 2.23.25; 3.25.3; 6.25.8). Luther would have

---

1 Jude has also been suspect since the earliest days because it appears to quote apocryphal books – the Assumption of Moses and Enoch – as Scripture (9, 14, 15).

dispensed with both Letters from his canon of Scripture. A modern scholar, E. F. Scott, says of II Peter that it is 'the least valuable of the NT writings'.[1]

That the two Letters are closely interdependent and must be taken together is clear. Of the 25 verses of Jude 19 appear in whole or in part in II Peter. The second chapter of II Peter includes almost everything in Jude 4-16. It is fairly certain that the writer of II Peter has incorporated Jude into his work almost entire.

It is further clear that both letters must be fairly late, for both look back to the beginnings of Christianity as if they were a long way away. Jude (3) speaks of the faith which was once for all delivered to the saints. II Peter (3.4) speaks of the fathers having fallen asleep. This is the way in which men speak when they are looking back on something which is now far past. When the Gnostics were propagating their beliefs, it was their habit to attach works to the great names of the past, as they did, for instance, in the case of the Gospel of Thomas or the Acts of John; and it may well be that both II Peter and Jude are Christian answers to these Gnostic claims, and that these little letters were issued by some part of the Church to say to the Gnostics what they were quite sure Jude and Peter would have said, if they had still been alive. Such a proceeding in the ancient world would have appeared perfectly natural, for often a disciple would write in the name of his master to say what he was certain that his master would have said. To speak of forgery in the modern sense of the term is a complete anachronism. Heretics and orthodox alike sought for their writings the lustre of the great names of the past.

Whatever we say of these writings, and whatever view we take of their origin, we could ill spare them from the NT, for they set before us a situation which threatened the Church like a deadly poison, and a situation which has kept recurring throughout the history of the Church. Jude certainly was written in a crisis. Its writer had intended to write a treatise on the Christian faith, but he had had to lay it aside to take up his pen to deal with this evil thing which had come into the life of the Church (3). Both letters are more invective than they are argument; their writers knew that there is a time when scathing condemnation is more effective than calm apologetic; and it is from the vivid and violent picture of the heretics that we must try to reconstruct what these heretics stood for.

I. They are not attacking the Church from outside; they are corrupting it from within. They are a blot on the love feasts of the Church (Jude 4; cp. II Peter 2.13; see RSV and NEB margin). Their conduct is such that they turn the *Agapē*, the Church's common meal of fellowship and love, into nothing better than a carousal and a revel. They have a defiling touch which makes the loveliest things unclean.

2. They deal in cleverly devised myths instead of the simplicity of the Gospel (1.16). This was typical of the Gnostics, who had to supply each of their aeons and their emanations with a genealogy and a history.

3. Their interpretations of Scripture were entirely subjective (1.20, 21). Instead of going to Scripture to find the true belief, they took their own twisted beliefs to Scripture and by the misuse of Scripture extracted from its justifications for their private beliefs. Instead of submitting to Scripture they made Scripture submit to them.

4. They brought discredit on the Church (2.2). Their way of life was such as to disgust men with the Church rather than to attract men to it.

5. They have taken upon themselves a fearful responsibility (2.21, 22). They cannot claim ignorance and lack of knowledge; they cannot plead that they have never had the chance to know the truth. They have known the right way and taken the wrong; they have heard the truth and have embraced a lie.

6. They have abandoned all belief in the Second Coming (3.4, 8-10). They have forgotten that, if God delays his hand, it is to give men the opportunity to repent, not to allow them licence to sin. But the Day of the Lord is inevitably on its way and will burst upon them in destruction and in judgment.

7. But one thing above all stands out about them, the licentiousness of their lives. They are openly licentious (2.2); in their greed they exploit their fellow-Christians (2.3); boldly and wilfully they give free rein to their defiling passions (2.4-10); they are notorious for their revelry, their dissipation, their carousing, their adultery, in which they not only engage themselves, but into which they also entice others (2.12-16); so far from having any sense of shame, and so far from seeking to conceal what they do, they boast of their folly (2.18); they promise men freedom, but in point of fact all that they have to offer is slavery to sin and corruption (2.19, 20).

Here is a picture written at white heat of men who had made the most blatant immorality the deliberate policy of their lives. The strange thing is that this is a picture which continuously appears in glimpses all through the NT.

It is Paul's last warning to the elders of Ephesus that into the flock there will come men who are like wolves and will speak perverse things (Acts 20.29). There are those who serve, not the Lord, but their own appetites (literally, their own belly), and with fair and flattering words deceive the simple-minded (Romans 16.18). Behind I Corinthians 6.9-20 there lie the beliefs of those who saw no harm in sexual immorality. There are cunning men with craftiness and deceitful wiles ready to lead their fellow-Christians astray (Ephesians 4.14). There are those who teach that immorality and impurity and covetousness are of no importance (Ephesians 5.6). There are those who are the enemies of the Cross of Christ, whose god is their belly, and who glory in their shame (Philippians 3.19). There are those who have rejected conscience and made shipwreck of the faith (I Timothy 1.19). The Christian must avoid the godless chatter and contradictions of what is falsely called knowledge (I Timothy 6.20). There are evil men and impostors who go on from bad to worse, deceiving and deceived (II Timothy 3.13). There comes the time when people will not endure sound doctrine, but will get themselves teachers to suit themselves (II Timothy 4.3). There are people who profess to know God, but who deny him by their deeds, and who are detestable and disobedient and unfit for any good deed (Titus 1.16).

It is a formidable indictment of what was evidently a widespread line of thought and way of conduct. This is the belief which is known as Antinomianism. Antinomianism is that attitude of mind which holds that *all* law has been banished and abrogated for the Christian. It will quote such a saying of Paul as: 'Christ is the end of the law, that everyone who has faith may be justified' (Romans 10.4). J. M. Sterrett defines Antinomianism[2] as follows: 'In its widest sense the term is used to designate the doctrines of extreme fanatics who deny subjection to any law other than the subjective caprices of the empirical individual, though this individual is generally credited as the witness and interpreter of the Holy Spirit.' The term itself was invented by Luther in his controversy with Johannes Agricola. Agricola in his anxiety to conserve the principle of salvation by faith held that even the Ten Commandments are abrogated for the Christian. 'Art thou steeped in sin, an adulterer or a thief? If thou believest, thou art in salvation. All who follow Moses must go to the Devil. To the gallows with Moses!'

This antinomianism was a characteristic feature of Gnostic teaching, and it issued in the most deliberate and licentious

2 In his article on it in Hastings' *Encyclopaedia of Religion and Ethics*.

immorality. The Gnostics allowed this immorality on three grounds: (i) Spiritual things are provided for the spiritual nature and carnal things for the carnal nature; the carnal nature legitimately and properly expresses itself in the things of the flesh. (ii) If gold be dipped in filth, it does not lose its beauty but retains its own nature; the filth has no power to injure the gold. Nothing that a spritual man can do can injure his spiritual substance. (iii) Since the Gnostic believed that only spirit is good and that matter is essentially evil, then he must long for the day when he will become pure spirit. That can only happen when a man has gone through every possible experience in life; he must experience life in its totality, even if he has to be reincarnated again and again to do so. Therefore it is a plain duty to seek the very depths of human experience, for the sooner they are experienced, the sooner release will come (Irenaeus' exposition of the doctrines of Valentinus and Carpocrates, *Against Heresies* 1.6; 1.25). Oddly enough, in Cromwellian times this same doctrine is found in the highest kind of Calvinism. If a man is elected and predestined to salvation, nothing can stop him being saved. However sinful he may be, and however wicked his actions, he needs neither confession nor repentance, for he will inevitably be saved.

Still another feature of this line of thought appears in Jude. We have already seen in our examination of the principles of Gnosticism that the Gnostics believed that the world was created by an inferior god, ignorant of, and hostile to, the true God. Not infrequently they took a further step and identified this hostile and ignorant god with the God of the Old Testament, who is said to have created the world. Now, if the God of the Old Testament is in fact a god ignorant of, and hostile to, the true God, then it follows that the people whom the God of the Old Testament approved are the bad people, and the people he condemned are the good people. Hence there was a sect of the Gnostics called the Ophites, who worshipped the serpent; and there were some who made Cain and Balaam and Korah the saints of Old Testament times (Jude II). Here in fact is the very essence of Gnosticism, for Gnosticism ended, as Clement of Alexandria put it, by deifying the Devil (*The Miscellanies* 4.12, 87). Gnosticism in effect turned morality upside down.

Here was the threat which beset the Church when II Peter and Jude were written. It was terrifyingly easy to pervert the Christian offer of salvation. Faith could be twisted into material for an argument that conduct was of no importance. Grace could be misinterpreted to mean that sin did not matter. Gnostic teaching, with its emphasis on spirit and its condemnation of matter, came preaching either that it did not matter what a man does with his body, or that it was nothing less than a duty to give the fleshly nature its full sway. It is easy to see how satanically attractive such teaching could be; and it is easy to see how those who propagated it would take to themselves a conscious superiority, contemptuous of those who still allowed themselves to be shackled and constricted by obedience to the moral law or to any other kind of law.

It is for this very reason that in II Peter Jesus is called Savior oftener than in any book in the NT (1.1; 2.20; 3.2; 3.18); and it is for this very reason that men are summoned to remember that the day comes when they will give account to him. It is for this reason that we can never spare from the NT the two little books which in white-hot holy anger see the literally damnable nature of any teaching which makes sin attractive, and which glorify Jesus Christ, not as the one who gives licence to sin, but as the one who is able to keep us from falling and to present us without blemish before the presence of the glory of God with rejoicing (Jude 24).

10
The Revelation

The Gospel of the Victor Christ

The Revelation is a book which has had a troubled history in the Church. F. V. Filson says of it that of all the NT books the Revelation seems to have aroused the most persistent protests, when the NT was being built up. There are only three uncial manuscripts which contain its text in full. It was not even translated into Syriac until late in the fifth century, and in that Church as late as the fourteenth century Ebedjesu does not list it among the books of the NT. There is no such thing as a Greek commentary on the Revelation until the fifth or sixth century. Luther would have none of it. 'I hold it', he said, 'to be neither apostolic nor prophetic. . . . My spirit cannot acquiesce in the book. I abide by the books which present Christ pure and clear.' 'After all, in it Christ is neither taught nor acknowledged.' Zwingli unequivocally rejected it: 'With the Apocalypse we have no concern, for it is not a biblical book. . . . The Apocalypse has no savor of the mouth or mind of John. I can, if I so will, reject its testimonies.'

The main objection to the Revelation has always been on the ground of its unintelligibility. The Apocalypse, said Jerome, has 'as many mysteries as words' (*Letters* 53.9). A despairing scholar said that the study of the Revelation either finds a man mad or leaves him so. H. B. Swete relates how he heard Benson tell of the answer of an intelligent reader to the question, 'What is the form the book presents to you?' The answer was, 'It is chaos'.

The result is that in modern times the Revelation has either been completely neglected, or it has become the playground of the religious eccentrics in their attempts to draw out time schedules of the last days.

That all this should have been so is a great pity, for to dispense with the Revelation would be to leave an unfillable gap in the literature of the NT; and, although many of its details must remain wrapped in mystery, its general message is clear, and it is a message which, especially in days of trouble, the Church can never do without. The Revelation itself claims to be two things, things which are closely inter-related and which are nonetheless essentially different.

The Revelation claims to be *prophecy*. The command to John is to prophesy (10.11). It is the God of the holy prophets who sends his angel with the message (22.6). The angel speaks to John of his brothers the prophets (22.9). The book is the book of prophecy and its words are the sayings of prophecy (22.7, 10, 18, 19). This in itself is a great enough claim, for the Jews sadly believed that the voice of prophecy had been silent for four hundred years. 'We do not see our signs; there is no longer any prophet, and there is none among us who knows how long' (Psalm 74.9). In I Maccabees decisions are repeatedly left until a prophet should come 'and tell us what to do' (I Maccabees 4.46; 9.27; 14.41). With the coming of the Christian Church prophecy was reborn (Acts 2.15-17; 11.28; 13.1; 15.32; Romans 12.6; I Corinthians 12.28; I Thessalonians 5.20; Ephesians 4.11). And it so happens that the Revelation is the only book claiming to be Christian prophecy that we possess.

But the Revelation is also a self-styled *Apocalypse*. The word translated *Revelation* is *apokalupsis*, which literally means a drawing aside of the veil to disclose some hidden sight. It is like the opening of the curtain on some drama, but the drama in question is not a man-made play but God-made history.

We often think of the Revelation as a quite unique book with nothing else like it; but it is of the first importance to remember that in fact the Revelation is the one representative in the NT of a type of literature called apocalyptic literature which was very common between the Testaments and in NT times. There are a large number of these Revelations or Apocalypses, both Jewish and Christian, still extant. All of them deal with the same situation. The Jews never lost their sense of being the chosen people, nor did they ever lose the confidence that some day God would openly and in the eyes of the world vindicate his own people. In the early days the dream was that that vindication would take place through the triumphant exploits of a king of David's line; the champion was a human champion and the victory was in time and in the world. As the centuries went on, the Jews came to feel that the forces of evil had become so dominant that this vindication could never come by human means. The only way in which it could ever come was by the direct and divine intervention of God. So, as we have seen before, the Jews came to have a standard time scheme. There is this present age, which is wholly bad, which is under the complete domination of evil, and from which God has withdrawn; the world is abandoned to the Devil. There will be the age which is to come, which will be wholly good, and wherein God will be King over all without a rival left to dispute his universal sway; and in this golden age the people of God will come into their own. But, as we have said, the Jewish thinkers had long since abandoned all hope that this might happen by any human means, and so between the two ages they placed the Day of the Lord. That would be the day when God broke directly into history with supernatural power which no man could resist. That day had in Jewish thought three main characteristics. It would come suddenly and unexpectedly, like a thief in the night. It would shatter the world; the sun would be turned into darkness and the moon into blood; it would be the end of things as they are now. It would be a time of judgment in which the wicked and the enemies of God would be obliterated and annihilated. The result would be the new world, the world of God.

All Apocalypses tell what is to happen in the terrible time between. They are all visions of the end time. For that very reason all Apocalypses are unintelligible in detail, for they are trying to draw a supernatural picture in natural terms. They are trying to tell of things which the eye has not seen and the ear has not heard and which have not entered into the mind of man. They are all trying to say the unsayable, to express the inexpressible, to describe the indescribable, to depict the unpaintable, to put into words divine, supernatural events which there are no words to describe. If then both prophecy and apocalyptic are trying to describe the future, what is the difference between them? In what follows we are drawing on the works of many writers.

1. Prophecy is *theistic*; apocalyptic is *deistic*. That is to say, the prophets see God in control of the world, but still present in the world and involved in the world; the apocalyptists see God as withdrawn from the world and acting on the world from outside.

2. In prophecy there is no thought that God is limited and frustrated by another divine power of evil. The cause of all the trouble is the misuse of the free will of man. In apocalyptic the revolt has reached heaven, and the Devil, Satan, Antichrist has become a personal power, disputing the dominion of the world with God.

3. To the prophets the reformation of all things was to come within this world; it was this world which was to be remade and recreated. To the apocalyptists this world was fit for nothing but total destruction, and the golden age would come only when

this world had disintegrated into nothingness and a new world had been created.

4. In prophecy the Messiah is ordinarily a human champion of the line of David; in apocalyptic the Messiah is a divine, supramundane, heavenly figure, who will break into the world from the outside.

5. Normally, with the single exception of our own NT Apocalypse, all apocalyptic books are pseudonymous. That is to say, they are written under the names of great figures of the past, such as Moses, Isaiah, Baruch, Enoch. There is something pathetic here. The prophet spoke in his own name and in the name of God; but the apocalyptist knew that he was second-rate, that he was derivative and not original, that he was living in an age when the stream of inspiration had run dry.

6. Apocalyptic is always literary; prophecy was delivered face to face by word of mouth to the people. Apocalyptic belongs to the library rather than the market-place, and smells of the lamp.

7. E. F. Scott makes the interesting point that apocalyptic is irresponsible. The prophet was involved in some definite situation; what he was demanding and pleading for was action here and now; he had to justify what he said in immediate contemporary action. The apocalyptist is a student or theologian shut up in his ivory tower with no chance of being called to put his visions into concrete social and political action.

8. In the nature of things prophecy is always highly practical; equally in the nature of things apocalyptic is highly speculative. Prophecy is about sin and repentance, action and decision, here and now in the human situation; apocalyptic is about wars in heaven, divine actions and purposes, and events of a future beyond time. The result is, as E. F. Scott says, that the atmosphere of the prophetic writings is vivid, concrete,

historical, while the atmosphere of the apocalyptic writings is abstract, rarefied, symbolic and remote from everyday life.

So then apocalyptic is basically a dream of a future when God will break into time and remake the world. Now one thing is clear – such a dream would inevitably be most vivid when the present was most bitter. It would be when life was an agony that men would turn their longing eyes to the future intervention of God. Is there then any desperate situation towards the end of the first Christian century which would explain how our Apocalypse came to be written, a situation from which men looked away to the ultimate triumph of God and of the people of God?

Sometime between AD 80 and 90 just such a situation emerged in the Christian Church. In the Revelation we come upon a completely new phenomenon. In the rest of the NT there is respect for the Roman government. Jesus had told men to render to Caesar what was Caesar's and to God what was God's (Matthew 22.15-22). Paul was a Roman citizen and proud of it. He was perfectly prepared to use the rights his citizenship gave him (Acts 21.39; 16.37-39). He counseled respect for the state as divinely appointed and the Christian Church was ordered to pray for the state and its leaders (Romans 13.1-7; I Timothy 2.2). Peter's instruction was to fear God and to honor the king (I Peter 2.17). But in the Revelation there is a complete *volte-face*. There emerges a blazing burning hatred of Rome; Rome is Babylon, the scarlet woman, the great harlot, drunk with the blood of the saints and the martyrs (14.8; 17.1-6). The hope and the prayer of the John of the Revelation is for the complete and total destruction of Rome. What had happened?

The answer is the emergence of compulsory Caesar worship. As far back as 195 BC the process began which was to end in the head-on collision between the Roman Empire and the Christian Church. In that year in the city of Smyrna there was erected the first temple of the divinity of Rome. This was no compulsory thing; it was completely spontaneous. Rome brought to these provincials such even-handed and impartial justice, such peace, safety and security, as under selfish and capricious tyrants they had never known. They felt that there was something divine about a power which could rule like that, and so the temple was erected to the spirit of Rome.

But something was thereby started which had a long way to go. The spirit of Rome, the divinity of Rome, was clearly centered and incarnated in one man. Many a time in the far away days earthly heroes on their death had been elevated to the rank of deity. And so there came another step in 29 BC, for in that year a temple was erected in Ephesus to the godhead of Julius Caesar after his death. First, the spirit of Rome had been deified; then the dead Emperor had been deified; and then almost exactly at the same time there came the last step. In Pergamum there was erected a temple, not to a dead Emperor, but to the living Augustus; and Emperor-worship had begun.

The early Emperors found this something of an embarrassment. They were very hesitant to accept this honor that was being forced upon them, and for long they allowed it in the East, but forbade it in the West. And then towards the end of the first century the process was complete. The great need of the far-flung Roman Empire was some unifying principle, something which would weld that heterogeneous conglomeration of nations into one. That unifying principle was found in Caesar-worship. It became 'the keystone of the imperial policy'. It became something like what the crown is in the British Commonwealth of nations; it became that which held the empire together. In the end it became necessary for every citizen of Rome to come to a stated place in his district on a certain day, burn his pinch of incense to the godhead of Caesar, and say: 'Caesar is Lord'.

It must clearly be noted that this was in essence far more a demonstration of political loyalty than of religious worship; and it must still more clearly be noted that Rome was the reverse of intolerant, and, if a man made this confession of political faith, he could then go away and worship any god he liked, so long as that worship did not conflict with public decency and order. All a man had to do was to say: 'Caesar is Lord.'

This is the one thing on earth no Christian would do. No Christian would take the name Lord and give it to anyone other than Jesus Christ. The result was that the Christians were regarded as dangerously disaffected citizens, as possible revolutionaries, as enemies of the state. And so the stage was set for the greatest battle in history. The choice was clear – Caesar or Christ? The Church with its humble people and its slaves was face to face with the might of Rome against which no power on earth had ever stood. As Sir William Watson wrote:

> So to the wild wolf Hate was sacrificed
> The panting, huddled flock, whose crime was Christ.

Here was the terrible situation with which the Church was faced, a situation in which humanly speaking the Church was doomed.

The Revelation has another connection with Rome. The beginning of the Roman persecution of the Christian Church had a certain almost accidental quality about it. It was due to the action of Nero, that Emperor whose name has become a synonym for infamy, and who to pagan and Christian alike seemed an unholy monster. On 19th July AD 64 the great fire of Rome broke out and it raged for a week, destroying alike the most sacred buildings and the homes of the common people, and leaving the people of Rome bound together in a community of misery. It was impossible to convince the citizens of Rome that Nero himself had not been responsible for the fire, for he had a passion for building and it was his ambition to rebuild Rome. In an effort to divert suspicion from himself Nero pinned the crime on to the Christians. Not even the Romans themselves believed that the Christians were really responsible, but the persecution was of the utmost savagery. Nero sowed up the Christians alive in the skins of beasts and set his hunting dogs to tear them in pieces. He rolled them still alive in pitch, and then used them as living torches to light his gardens. The sheer cruelty of the Neronic persecution left an indelible impression on the minds of the Christians.

In due time in AD 68 Nero's reign came to an end in utter chaos. It was said that the people danced in the streets at the news that Nero was dead. But soon a rumor was sweeping the city and the country; it was said that Nero was not dead; he seemed immortal in his wickedness; it was said that he had gone to Parthia to wait there and that he was soon to descend on Rome from Parthia with the Parthian hordes. This belief came to be known as the *Nero Redivivus*, the Nero Resurrected, legend. It was so powerful a legend that in AD 69, 80 and even as late as 88 pretenders claiming to be the Nero Redivivus arose in Parthia.

Now by this time Christianity had come to think in terms of Antichrist, the figure who was the supreme opponent of God, God's enemy in the universe; and not unnaturally the Nero Redivivus legend and the Antichrist conception became entangled together. Such had been the cruelty of Nero, to such an extent had Nero acquired the reputation of being the scourge of the Church and the antagonist of God that he became identified with Antichrist. We get this specially in the picture of the Beast in the notorious thirteenth chapter of the Revelation. The beast from the sea (13.1) is Caesar-worship invading Asia Minor. The seven heads are the seven Emperors to whom

Caesar-worship had been given up to that time, Tiberius, Caligula, Claudius, Nero, Vespasian, Titus and Domitian. After the death of Nero there had been some months of chaos in which three Emperors had reigned for brief periods, Galba, Otho and Vitellius. They with the seven others make up the ten horns. The blasphemous name on the heads is *kurios*, lord, the title which belonged only to Christ and which the Roman Emperors blasphemously claimed. One of the heads had a mortal wound that had been healed. That head (13.2, 12) is the worst of all and that head stands for Nero wounded to death and resurrected, Nero Redivivus, Antichrist. The number of the beast is 666 (13.18), and that is the sum total of the letters in the name Nero Caesar in Hebrew, when the letters are taken as numbers. (Greek and Hebrew had no signs for the numbers, and the letters stood for the numbers, as if in English a = 1, b = 2, c = 3, and so on.) Such was the reputation of Nero and so strong was the Nero Redivivus legend that Nero was identified with Antichrist and with the Beast.

So then the Revelation was written at a time when the might of Rome was rising up to crush the Church, and when an Antichrist who was a reincarnation of Nero was expected to come. That time was in fact the reign of the Emperor Domitian. We have already seen that the early Roman Emperors were more than half embarrassed by the rise of Caesar-worship, but not so Domitian (AD 81-96). He demanded it; he liked the crowd to greet him like a god when he entered the amphitheatre; he began all his edicts, 'Domitian, Lord and God, commands'. He was not like Nero a man of sudden rages; he was rather a cold-blooded, calculating eliminator of all who stood in his way. On the face of it, it was difficult to see what could save the Christian Church. If we remember this situation, the whole atmosphere of the Revelation becomes dramatically intelligible. Let us then turn to the book itself.

So far from bringing chaos, the Revelation follows a carefully wrought dramatic pattern. It falls into seven parts.

1. There is the Prologue in chapter 1, which tells of the situation in the life of John in which the book was written.

2. There are chapters 2 and 3 in which the seven Churches are urged to put their houses in order before the storm burst and the crucial struggle began.

3. In chapters 4 and 5 the scene shifts to heaven, and the seer is granted in his vision admission to the presence of God.

4. In heaven the book of destiny is opened. We are, as it were, given a preview of history in advance; and the history which we are allowed in symbol to see is that of the terrible end-time between the two ages, the birth-pangs and the prelude to the new heaven and the new earth. It is therefore history in a series of cataclysmic disasters. There are the seven seals and their opening, with a fresh disaster at each opening (6.1-17). There are the seven trumpet blasts, each bringing some new terror (8.1-13; 9.1-21; 13.15-19). There are the seven bowls, the pouring out of which brings a series of terrible things (16.1-21). It is as if John heaped together every terrible thing in one composite picture of awfulness. The scene shifts and we see war in heaven, in which the Devil is cast out and comes to earth (12). Then the Beast comes to the earth and does his dreadful work (13).

5. We are now coming near to the end of the drama. There comes the defeat of the Beast (17.19-21). There comes the temporary defeat and binding of the power of evil, which is followed by the Millennium, the thousand-year reign of the martyred saints with Christ, an idea found only in the Revelation (20.1-6).

6. At the end of the Millennium there is one grand conflict to end all conflicts. The forces of evil are conquered; the Devil is flung into the lake of fire; and there follow the general resurrection and the final judgment (20.7-15).

7. Finally, there is the picture of the new heaven and the new earth (21.1-8), and in particular of the new Jerusalem (21.9-22.5).

So the dramatic progress through tragedy into triumph, through death into life, is depicted.

It is necessary that we should stop to look at one part of this picture, the picture of the Millennium, for it has often played, and often still plays, a quite disproportionate part in Christian thought.

1. Two things are to be noted. The Revelation (20.1-6) is the only book in the NT which knows anything about it, and even there it appears in only a few verses. Second, the Millennium affects, according to the Revelation, only those who have died as martyrs (20.4); others will remain asleep until the general resurrection.

2. Where did Millenarianism or Chiliasm (*chilios* is the Greek for a thousand) come from? Millenarianism was strongest where the Church was most Jewish. Jewish eschatology is fluid, and, although the general view is that the reign of the Messiah will last for ever, there are parts of it in which the Messiah has a limited reign. Enoch sees history as a series of weeks. There are seven weeks of the world as it is; in the eighth week there is the week of the righteous in which the righteous are given a sword to destroy their enemies, and the house of God is built. In the ninth week the wicked are written down for destruction; in the tenth week there comes the judgment and only after that the final blessedness. In that time-scheme the eighth and ninth weeks correspond to the Millennium. II Esdras (7.28, 29) fixes the Messianic reign at four hundred years, after which the Messiah will die. The four hundred years is arrived at by combining Genesis 15.13 and Psalm 90.15. Abraham is told that Israel's affliction will last for four hundred years; the Psalmist prays: 'Make us glad as many

days as thou hast afflicted us, and as many years as we have seen
evil.' Therefore the period of bliss must be also four hundred
years. Commonest of all was the idea that the age of the world
would correspond to the time taken for creation. The time
taken for creation was held to be six thousand years, since a day
with the Lord is as a thousand years and a thousand years as a
day (Psalm 90.4; II Peter 3.8). The world would therefore last
for six thousand years and the seventh thousand would be the
Sabbath, the reign of the Messiah. This is almost exactly
Millenarianism. There can be little doubt that Millenarianism
can be traced back to Jewish eschatology.

3. Millenarianism was never a universally accepted belief of
the Church. It was too often conceived of in very material
terms. It was in fact objected against Cerinthus that he looked
for a Millennium 'of desires and pleasures and marriage
festivals, delights of the belly and sexual passion, eating and
drinking and marrying'. The Millenium could become
perilously near a Mohammedan paradise. Origen rebuked such
views, saying that in heaven we would indeed eat, but we would
eat the bread of life; we would indeed drink, but we would
drink the cup of wisdom. Augustine, who had originally been a
literal Millenarianist, dealt Millenarianism what was almost its
death-blow, at least as part of the main stream of the belief of
the Church. He came to see the binding of Satan as the binding
of the strong man (Mark 3.27; Luke 11.22); the thousand years
as the time between the first advent and the final conflict; the
first resurrection as the resurrection which the Christian shares
with Christ in baptism.

Millenarianism has never been a fully integrated part of the
belief of the Church. Almost certainly it is a survival from
Jewish eschatology. Anything in the Revelation must in any
event be interpreted symbolically. To stress it literally is to seek
to found a doctrine on a few verses of Scripture and to neglect

the main stream of NT teaching. It must be said that
Millenarianism belongs rather to the eccentricities of Christian
theology.

There are many who have been quite out of sympathy with
the theology of the Apocalypse. Even F. V. Filson describes the
Revelation as being 'off the Gospel center'. H. B. Swete says:
'No one who comes to the Apocalypse fresh from the study of
the Gospels and Epistles can fail to recognize that he has passed
into another atmosphere.' E. F. Scott says: 'He (John) has
nothing to say about love, humility, forgiveness. He frankly
hated his enemies and rejoiced in their downfall. In the whole
course of the book we can catch hardly a distant echo of the
Sermon on the Mount. . . . From the Revelation it could never
have been gathered that Jesus was compassionate, that he healed
the sick and encouraged the helpless and outcast and bore our
infirmities, that he was meek and lowly of heart. . . . As we
know him from this book, Christ is a great but terrible figure,
righteous but implacable, the champion of his people, but
breathing destruction on his enemies.' Christ is the Christ of the
sharp-two-edged sword (1.14-16); Christ is the Christ of the
sickle wherewith the earth is reaped (14.14-16); Christ is the
rider on the white horse wading through the blood of his
enemies (19.11-16). God is never said to love anyone, not even
the Christians. He is might and majesty and power (15.3, 4);
and the sinner will drink the wine of his wrath and fury which
go out against men (14.10, 19; 15.7; 19.15). And yet it must be
remembered that this also is the God who wipes the tear from
every eye (7.17).

And yet it remains true that to criticize the Revelation
harshly is to show a curious lack of historical insight and a
complete lack of sympathy. The Revelation was written is a time
when the might of Rome had risen to crush the Christian
Church. No one had ever withstood the ineluctable might of

Rome. What possible defence could these poor, humble Christians, without money, without social standing, without earthly wisdom, without political influence, find against the flood-tide of the majesty of Rome? The John of the Revelation answers in one word – God.

The most characteristic title for God in the Revelation is *pantokratōr*, which quite literally means *in control of everything*. That word is used of God eight times in the Revelation and only once in the rest of the NT, and that in a quotation from the OT (Revelation 4.8; 11.17; 15.3; 16.7, 14; 19.6, 15; 21.22; II Corinthians 6.18). The battle-cry of the Revelation is: 'Hallelujah! For the Lord our God the Almighty reigns' (19.6). It is as if the Christian in all his defencelessness faced the Empire in all its might and said: 'You think that you have the last word. You have not. The last word belongs to God, and we and you and all the universe are in his control.' The John of the Revelation has laid hold on the majestic power of Almighty God, when there was no other defense. In other words, certainly the Revelation stresses the might of God, but that might is exercised in love for his people. Certainly the Revelation paints the picture of the warrior Christ, but it is not Jesus of Nazareth who is in John's mind; it is Jesus Christ, risen, ascended, glorified and willing and able to save his people against impossible odds. The Revelation preaches the Gospel of the Victor Christ with whom a man can face odds which would drive a Christless man to utter despair.

Before we leave the Revelation, let us ask one question. In view of the fact that there are many who would have discarded this book, are there any reasons why we must strenuously refuse to let it go?

1. The Revelation sees the whole universe as the scene of the battle between God and the Devil, between Christ and Antichrist, between good and evil, a struggle which will

continue to the end of time. It therefore lays before men, as few
NT books do, the necessity to decide for or against God. It asks
every man: 'On what side are *you*?'

2. The Revelation lays down the place of the Church in this
battle. The Church is in the front line. In heaven the battle has
been won and Satan has been cast out; but it still rages on earth;
and for the winning of it the strength and the purity of the
Church are essential. The Revelation is a call to Christian
commitment for the sake of God.

3. The Revelation lays it down above all else that God is in
control. Even when life is at its darkest and its most agonizing,
even when it seems that Christianity is in danger of extinction,
even when the forces of the world seem irresistibly strong, 'the
Lord God omnipotent reigneth'.

4. The Revelation therefore lays down the majestic
resources of the Christian in any time of trouble. Whatever
forces may be on the other side, the Christian has God. This
does not exempt a man from the struggle and the agony and the
cross; but it does mean that fidelity is the way to glory. That is
why in every time of trouble the Revelation has come again into
its own.

5. The Revelation is quite certain that history is going
somewhere. History is not a chaos; history is not a meaningless
jumble of events; history and destiny are one; and a man is faced
with the question: 'Are you in the way, or on the way?'

6. The Revelation lays it down that in spite of the place of
the Church in the scheme of things, in spite of the challenge to
the individual Christian, in the last analysis the end can only
come by the action of God. The ultimate victory can never be
man-won; it must always be God-given and God-achieved.

7. In view of all this the Revelation lays it down that heaven
is more important than earth, and time than eternity. It is not
what happens on earth that is important, but what happens in

heaven when earth is done. And it is for that very reason that a man must accept the blood and sweat and tears of the human situation. A man's duty is never to seek survival, but always to seek life.

There are doubtless many things in the Revelation which defy understanding, but the central truth remains crystal clear – Christ is the Victor Christ.

11
The Kērugma

The Essence of the Gospel

So far we have been thinking of the diversity of the Gospel, and we have been seeing how each of the NT writers had his own grasp and experience and expression of the Gospel; but behind the diversity there is a unity. The area in which the diversity moves is not unlimited; the diversity is the expression of a common essence of the faith.

To that essence of the Gospel the name *kērugma* has been given. The noun *kērugma* is connected with the verb *kērussein* which in turn describes the work and the function of the *kērux*. It is this last word which gives us the real key to what the *kērugma* is. *Kērux* is the Greek for a *herald*; *kērussein* means *to proclaim as a herald proclaims*; *kērugma* is such a *proclamation*. The *kērugma* is then the basic proclamation of the Gospel. It is that essence of the Gospel about which there is no argument. It will have to be explained; it will have to be expounded; it will have to be systematized; it will have to be worked out and applied in life and living; it will have to be conceptualized until it becomes theology. But the *kērugma* itself is that basic statement of the Gospel which is proclamation and about which there is no argument. It is the foundational statement of the faith of which a man says: 'This is what I believe, and it is from this that I start.'

Let us then examine this basic message, this unity which lies behind the rich diversity of NT thought.[1]

1. *The crisis of history has arrived; the prophecies are fulfilled; and the Age to Come has begun.*

Right at the beginning we must remember that the earliest Christian *kērugma* is necessarily expressed in Jewish terms; it is the proclamation of men who were Jews, and whose whole background was the Old Testament, and its design was to convince Jews of the truth of Christianity. This first statement of the *kērugma* arises from a basic line of Jewish thought which we have noted before. The Jews by NT times divided all history into two ages. There was *this present age*, wholly bad, wholly under the domination of Satan, incurable, unreformable, irremediable, destined for nothing but total destruction and obliteration. There was the *age to come*, which was the age of God and the reign of God, and in which the world and all that is in it was to become new. So then this initial statement of the *kērugma* lays down three things.

(*a*) With the coming of Jesus Christ something new has happened. The coming of Jesus Christ does not mean simply an alteration, or adjustment, or even a reformation of the existing order. A government may, for instance, reshuffle its cabinet, but nothing really new has been brought it. A government may introduce new policies and new measures, but they are aimed at the reformation of an already existing order of things. But with the coming of Jesus Christ something totally new has happened.

---

1 The definition of the *kērugma* is connected with the name of the English New Testament scholar Dr C. H. Dodd, and in particular with his book *The Apostolic Preaching and its Developments*. The application of the *kērugma* to the various strands of NT thought was further worked out by Dr A. M. Hunter in his book *The Unity of the New Testament*. The actual statement of the *kērugma* which we propose to take as a basis for our consideration of it is taken from Dr Dodd's commentary on *The Johannine Epistles* in the Moffatt Commentary (p. xxviii).

Into life there has come something which did not exist before, and which without him could not exist; and that something is not something which has emerged from the human situation; it is something which has entered life from outside, from God.

(*b*) In spite of that, this something is connected with the past. It is the fulfilment of all the hopes and dreams and visions which the Spirit of God has put into the minds and hearts of men in all the ages of the past. Although it has come from outside history, it is nevertheless that towards which all history has been moving. It is the event in which all human, but divinely inspired, hopes and dreams find their realization and in which history finds its consummation. It does not grow out of the past, and yet without the past it could not have happened. It is the coming of that power which realizes the hopes and dreams which could never become actualized until the new power entered into life and into the world.

(*c*) The result of this coming of Jesus is a new kind of life. It is not primarily a new kind of knowledge. It is a new kind of living. It is not primarily a new way of knowing, although it is good news about God. It is primarily a new way of living, the bringing into life of a new quality, which could never have humanly emerged and which had to be divinely given and inspired.

2. *Jesus of Nazareth, of the line of David, came as God's Son, the Messiah.*

The place of Jesus in this new scheme of things is not simply that of the great leader or reformer or even prophet. His place is that he is God acting in the world, God entering into the human situation, eternity invading time. He is not to be explained in human terms, nor is he to be expressed in human categories; he is to be explained and expressed in terms of God. He is more than even the messenger and the instrument of God; he is God entering into the human situation in order to change it as only God can change it. To that end certain statements can be made of Jesus.

(*a*) *He did mighty works.* To the human situation he brings *power*, power to deal with the sin, the sorrow, the suffering of the human situation. He does not simply bring a message or a new kind of knowledge; he brings a new kind of power, which can be seen in visible action, which is able to meet and to defeat the results and the consequences of the sin of man.

(*b*) *He gave a new and authoritative teaching or law.* To the human situation he brings *authority*, such authority that he can look back on the ancient pronouncements of the Law, show their inadequacy, and then say: 'But I tell you . . .' (Matthew 5.22, 28, 34, 39, 44). With him there is no expressing of an opinion or the suggestion of a possibility; he needs to cite no authority; he needs to qualify none of his statements with the proviso that he may be mistaken. He speaks the last and final word on life and living. In him men are confronted with what to believe and how to live – and there is no argument.

(*c*) *He was crucified, dead and buried for our sins.* This too was the fulfilment of prophecy, however paradoxical and impossible the idea of a crucified Messiah might seem to Jewish thought. So to the ideas of power and authority there is added the idea of *sacrifice*. Jesus in his life and his death paid in full the cost which was necessary to set right the human situation.

(*d*) *He rose again the third day.* Here is the idea of *victory*. Jesus rose victorious over the worst that sin could do to him, and in the end conquered even death. It is the simple fact that in the early Church it was not so much the crucified Christ as the risen Christ that the early preachers preached. They never preached a sermon without insisting on the fact of the resurrection (Acts 2.24; 3.15; 4.10; 5.31; 10.40; 13.30; 17.3, 31; 26.23). It was with the figure of the victorious and the ever-living Christ that they confronted men. The preachers of the early Church would have felt that a message which stopped at the Cross had omitted the greatest fact of all, the fact of the resurrection.

(*e*) *He was exalted to the right hand of God.* Here is the idea of the *glory* of Jesus Christ. Jesus Christ is crucified and crowned. After suffering on earth he reigns in glory. He is not only risen; he is the risen Lord.

(*f*) *He will come again as Judge of the quick and the dead.* The message was a message that history was going somewhere, that it was not simply dragging endlessly on, that it was not a circular repetition, that it was not a series of chance and unconnected events, but that it was a process moving towards a consummation. That consummation was to be the return of Jesus Christ as Judge, and the establishment of God as Lord over all. Here we have the idea of the final *lordship* of Jesus Christ.

So the *kērugma* presented men with a statement of the power and of the authority of Jesus Christ, of his sacrifice, his victory, his glory and his final lordship.

3. *The apostles and those in fellowship with them constitute the Church, the New Israel of God, marked out as such by the outpouring of the Spirit.*

Here there are by implication certain basic facts about the life of the Christian.

(*a*) The Christian is called to life in a community. Christianity is not simply a matter between a man and God. It is not simply a relationship between a man and Jesus Christ. It is also a relationship between a man and his fellow-men. The new life is based not on individualism but on fellowship.

(*b*) That community is in the world but it is different from the world. Its difference is to be expressed not by withdrawal from the world but by living in the world; and part of its duty is to transform the world in which it lives. It is a community which has a threefold responsibility – a responsibility to Jesus Christ, a responsibility to the fellow-members of the community, and a responsibility to those who are as yet outside the community.

(*c*) The idea of a 'chosen people' remains, but the idea of that which constitutes the 'chosenness' is radically altered. The Jews interpreted the idea of the chosen people in a racial sense. For them to be a member of the chosen people was to be a circumcised Jew. Stated in its crudest form, as indeed it sometimes was, this meant that a Jew needed nothing other than his Jewishness to be in a specially favored relationship to God. But now the chosen people are all those who have accepted Jesus Christ. The chosenness does not now consist in membership of any nation or in any external mark upon the body; it consists of a relationship to Jesus Christ. The chosen people are those of every race and nation who have taken Jesus Christ as Savior and Lord.

(*d*) The mark of the new community is the possession of the Spirit. Those within the new community should be recognizable by a new vitality and a new power and a new ability to deal with life and to cope with life which cannot be possessed by those who do not possess the Spirit.

4. *Therefore repent, believe in Christ, and you will receive forgiveness of sins, and a share in the life of the Age to come, or Eternal life.*

The *kērugma finishes* with three imperatives.

(1) There is the summons to *believe in Christ*. That is to say, there is the summons to accept the claim of Christ, to take him at his word and to believe that he can do what he has promised to do. To believe in Christ is to believe that his claim to a special and unique relationship to God is true, and that therefore he has the right to make the demands which he does make and the power to fulfil the promises which he has given.

(2) There is the summons *to repent*. Obviously, to accept the claims and the promises of Christ is to set out in a new direction. It is to face God instead of turning away from God; it is to change one's mind about life and to accept a new set of values for life; it is to effect, through the help of Christ, an ethical change in life, so that action and even thought become cleansed and purified.

(3) There is the summons *to accept*. That which is offered is the life of the Age to Come or eternal life. That is to say, what is offered is a foretaste here and now of the divine life of God. It is to find the beginning of heaven even in time.

Whatever be the diversity which we find in the New Testament, at the back of it there is the *kērugma*. The offer of the *kērugma*, and of the New Testament, is a faith which is centered in Christ, which issues in life, and which looks to eternity.

12
Preaching the New Testament Today

In any engagement it is always wise to see just what we are up against. What then is the situation which meets us when we try to preach the NT today? To put it in another way, what is the situation which faces us when we try to communicate the gospel, not so much to the people inside the Church as to the people outside the visible Christian fellowship?

(*a*) Unquestionably, we face *ignorance* of the basic facts of the Christian story. W. E. Sangster tells how in 1947 Admiral Sir Geoffrey Layton carried out an experiment with regard to the lads who in that year joined the Navy, and who, it must be assumed, must have been rather above the average in intelligence. Only 15 per cent could repeat the Lord's Prayer accurately; 28 per cent knew it in part; 49 per cent knew no more than the opening words. Although 72 per cent knew who Jesus Christ was, only 39 per cent knew where he was born. What happened on Good Friday was known to 62 per cent, but only 45 per cent knew the meaning of Easter, and only a little more than 2 per cent could explain Whitsuntide. From one point of view this ignorance is a handicap, because it means that we can assume little or nothing in our approach to people outside the Church. From another point of view it is an advantage, for it means that what we have to tell them is for them a new discovery.

(*b*) Equally unquestionably, we have to face a situation in which the Christian message and the Church have become to many a complete irrelevance. Fairly recently the *Sunday Post*, a newspaper which is entirely well-disposed to the Church and to religion, conducted an investigation into the reaction of young people to religion and to the Church. A nineteen-year-old clerk said: 'I don't believe in God. I don't believe in religion whatsoever.' A nineteen-year-old apprentice accountant said: 'Christianity is a thing of the past. It's dying out rapidly. I won't be sorry to see it go. Church? Not for me.' A nineteen-year-old science student said: 'Religion has no place in modern society. They repeat the same things over and over again.' The conviction of the irrelevance of the Church was equally marked. A twenty-year-old student said: 'The ideals the Church preaches are all right, but you don't need a Church to know how to behave.' A twenty-year-old art student said: 'I believe I can stay in contact with God without doing it publicly.' A lad of sixteen said: 'Church drives me up the wall. It's not worth getting out of bed for. None of my pals go to Church either.'

It has to be noted that in no case is there any particular hostility to the Church. There is complete indifference to an institution and a belief which has simply ceased to have any relevance.

Clearly, the next question is: What has the Christian preacher to offer to meet this situation?

He has his preaching, and it has been pointed out that there are four kinds of preaching. There is *kērugma*, which is the uncompromising statement of the facts of the Christian faith. This is proclamation without argument. There is *didachē*, which is the explanation of these facts, both as they are problems for the mind, and as they are matter of practical life and conduct. In other words, there is the development of the *kērugma* into Christian theology and Christian ethics. There is *paraklēsis*, which is exhortation to accept the Christian faith and to live the Christian life. There is *homilia*, which is the treatment of any subject in the light of the Christian message. Somewhere within these different spheres the Christian preacher will move.

Clearly, the next question is: What has gone wrong? Why is it that Christian preaching in so many cases is no longer effective? Certain causes are almost immediately identifiable even if we go no further than look at these four different kinds of Christian preaching.

(*a*) It is clear that somewhere the balance has gone wrong. There is any amount of *homilia*, the general treatment of almost any subject in the form of a kind of Christian and moral essay. There is an equally large, if not still greater, amount of *paraklēsis,* of the kind of exhortation which is a kind of Christian pep-talk. There is not a great deal of *kērugma*, for it is a strange feature of the Christian message today that it has become apologetic – in both senses of the word – rather than dogmatic – again in both senses of the term. But the real disaster of the situation is the absence of *didachē*, the neglect of the teaching ministry of the Church. One of the main faults of so much modern preaching is that it lives from day to day, looking each week for a 'good text', instead of being a systematic and planned exposition of the Christian faith and of the Bible. There is little good in exhorting people to be Christian, when they have no clear idea of what being Christian means.

(*b*) There is the use of religious jargon, or, to put it in another way, the use of conventional religious words and expressions without any definition of them. W. E. Sangster told how Dr William D. White carried out an experiment in which he asked twenty-five intelligent people in his congregation to make a list of words and phrases, commonly used in preaching, which they did not understand. The list included such words as dayspring, logos, husbandman, washed in the blood of the Lamb, cherubim and seraphim, throne of mercy, heir of salvation, alpha and omega, things of the flesh, balm in Gilead, the bosom of Abraham, in Christ. It may well be that there are many who fail to understand still greater phrases like the Kingdom of Heaven, justification by faith, sanctification, atonement, eternal life, simply because they are so often used but so seldom expounded and explained.

The great characteristic of the language and the thought of the NT is that it was completely contemporary. It is the simple linguistic fact that, apart from the papyri, the NT is the supreme monument of Hellenistic Greek, Greek as the ordinary man spoke it in the first century AD. And further, it is the supreme characteristic of the NT that it uses categories of thought which were completely familiar to the people to whom it spoke. And the problem which faces us today is precisely the problem of persuading ourselves to admit that these categories of thought are quite alien and strange to the mind of the twentieth century and have to be reminted and restated in the language and the thought of today. It may well be that it is a basic mistake of a great deal of the presentation of the Christian message that it is offered in first-century categories of Jewish and Hellenistic thought expressed in Elizabethan English.

(*c*) However much we may hesitate to say it, it has to be said that a great deal of modern preaching is essentially trivial in its nature. W. E. Sangster said that 'a great deal of Protestant preaching for a generation past has been on marginal things'. Bishop Kulandram, looking with oriental eyes on western preaching, said that what struck him most was 'its astonishing silence on deep theological issues'. When that famous preacher Leslie J. Tizard was dying, and when he was thinking of what preaching had to say to a man with incurable and inoperable cancer, he quoted a saying of J. B. Priestley that people get a bit sick of having the front of their minds tickled, when they want something 'which goes deeper'. A group of intelligent people deeply regretted that the older didactic and exegetical sermon has so much given place to the topical address.

Clearly, the next and the last question must be: In what direction lies the cure? It lies in three directions.

(*a*) It lies in a revival of expository preaching. To put it very bluntly, it is the fact that people are not very interested, at least they are not interested for long, in hearing any man's opinions about all kinds of things political, social and economic; they are interested in trying to find out what the Bible has to say. And it is there that the preacher can help them. He has been deliberately trained in linguistic, historical, archaeological, theological study in a way which enables him to discover the meaning of, and thus to expound, scripture in a way that is simply not open to the layman. The whole aim of his training is to do precisely that. It is in fact the one thing that he *can* do better than the layman. The first thing that is needed from all pulpits is systematic exposition of scripture and systematic explanation of Christian doctrine, with the application of both to the human situation of the particular sphere of the hearers in the twentieth century.

(*b*) It lies in an approach of sheer honesty. This will involve the abandonment of conventional religious language which has ceased to be meaningful even to the preacher. It will involve the refusal to mutter pious platitudes. It will involve the frank admission by the preacher that there are problems before which he can only stand silent and go on seeking. A reverent agnosticism can be on occasion a better evangelism than a religion which knows all the answers.

(*c*) It will involve a total approach to the New Testament. One of the worst of all mistakes is to standardize one religious experience, and to speak and to preach as if there were no other. The NT has its John and James as well as its Paul. The amazing thing about the NT is its frank admission that there are many ways to God, and the mistake which so many of us make, which maybe we all make, is to limit our preaching to that which specially appeals to ourselves. It is necessary to expound the full-orbed teaching of the New Testament, to remember that, while there is one Lord, there are many witnesses, and, when we set ourselves to do that we will undoubtedly find that parts of scripture which we thought had nothing to say to us become strangely and amazingly eloquent.

W. E. Sangster tells somewhere of the preacher who read himself full, thought himself clear, and prayed himself hot; and to read, to think and to pray is the only way to become a preacher in any century.